the leopard
and
the fox

tAriq Ali

the leopard and the fox

A PAKISTANI TRAGEDY

Seagull
BOOKS

london new york calcutta

Special paperback edition for sale in Pakistan only

Seagull Books

Editorial offices:

1st Floor, Angel Court, 81 St Clements Street,
Oxford OX4 1AW, UK

1 Washington Square Village, Apt 1U, New York,
NY 10012, USA

26 Circus Avenue, Calcutta 700 017, India

Seagull Books 2007

ISBN 1 9054 2 229 6

British Library Cataloguing-in-Publication Data
A catalogue record for this book is available from the British Library

Typeset by Seagull Books, Calcutta, India
Printed in Calcutta, India, at Ananda Palit Printers

CONTENTS

EXPLANATORY PREFACE

In September 1985 I was approached by Robin Midgley, Head of Drama at BBC, Pebble Mill, and commissioned to write a three-part drama series on the trial and execution of Pakistan's first elected Prime Minister, Zulfiqar Ali Bhutto, that followed the military coup carried out by General Zia-ul-Haq in 1977. I agreed. The three episodes of 'The Leopard and the Fox' were completed by January 1986 and submitted to the BBC. Robin Midgley began to discuss casting the principals and we agreed that Zia Mohyedin would play the General and that we would approach the Indian actor Naseerudin Shah to play Bhutto. Other approaches (e.g. Angelique Huston as Benazir Bhutto; Sian Thomas as Nusrat Bhutto) were still being discussed when all proceedings were halted.

The drama series had become 'controversial' within the BBC hierarchy: The Director-General, Alasdair Milne, had asked to read the scripts. As Editor-in-Chief of the Corporation, he had every right to do so, but it was still an unusual request. In those days, BBC Heads of Departments had an amazing degree of freedom and were rarely questioned, despite the presence of intelligence operatives within the Corporation. The fact that Milne had demanded to read the scripts was a sign that he was being 'nobbled from above.' Why? Because at the time General Zia-ul-Haq, the most brutal military dictator in Pakistan's history, was considered a vital and valued ally of the West in the 'struggle for freedom' in Afghanistan. He was the godfather of Osama Bin Laden and the jihadi guerrillas and Pakistani irregulars then fighting the Russians (and today NATO) in the mountains of Afghanistan. It was Zia who funded, armed and organized the armed Islamic groups that are still wreaking havoc in the region. But he was a tried, tested and trusted officer, who had been trained at Fort Bragg. It was he who had led Pakistani troops and Bedouins to crush the Palestinians in Jordan in September 1970. He was now considered essential for Washington's Afghan operation, backed to the hilt by Margaret Thatcher.

It was hardly surprising that the State Department and the British Foreign Office would frown on any attempt to destabilize Zia's dictatorship. That is why the Director-General of the BBC had asked to read the scripts.

A few weeks later Mark Tully, the veteran BBC journalist, based in Delhi, rang me up. He, too, had read the scripts and wanted to meet up for a drink to discuss them. I was advised by Robin Midgley to take this meeting very seriously and not be too provocative. Mark and I met at the Groucho Club in Soho and after exchanging a few pleasantries, he came straight to the point. He had been asked by Alasdair to read the scripts and liked the flavour, but there was ONE problem. I smiled politely. Tully said that in the third episode 'Two Men, One Coffin' I had alleged that the United States had green-lighted Bhutto's hanging. I pleaded guilty. 'I was in Rawalpindi at the time,' Tully told me, 'and I could find no evidence of US involvement.'

'You couldn't have looked very hard, Mark.'

I explained that the US Embassy and its Saudi surrogate were all-powerful in Zia's Pakistan and any senior military officer would confirm that Zia consulted them before hanging Bhutto. Tully disagreed. Finally he said:

'What if I were to tell you that if you took that section out of the series the BBC would definitely go ahead?'

'I would tell the BBC to fuck off!' was my thoughtful response.

That was the end. The funeral rites were administered by J. P. Coman, a BBC inhouse Deputy Solicitor who informed Robin Midgley and myself that the project was definitely off.

'Why?' asked Midgley politely.

'Because of the libel risk.'

'What of all the dramas on British TV that regularly libel the Soviet politburo and its Eastern European adjuncts?' I asked him.

'Do you think a British judge would award damages to the Soviet politburo?'

'And do you think a British judge would award damages to a squalid, third-rate military dictator with blood on his hands?'

Mr Coman did not reply. His views as expressed in writing are available as Appendix B.

The script published here is a shortened version that was prepared from a Channel Four project—'The Assassination Quartet'—dealing with the deaths of Solomon Bandaranaike (Ceylon), Bhutto, Indira Gandhi and Sheikh Mujibur Rehman (Bangladesh). This project was never filmed because of financial shortfalls, not political censorship.

I have left this final version of the script unchanged. As a result there is an event described here which has subsequently been denied. At the time of writing, rumours were rife that Bhutto had died before he was hanged. Subsequently, most of the people involved have denied that this was the case. Apart from that, the script remains a fairly accurate if unhappy reminder of two tragedies: Bhutto's failure to transform the country and Zia's well-planned brutalization of Pakistan's political culture, the effects of which are visible every single day.

Tariq Ali
August 2006

THE LEOPARD AND THE FOX

Scene 1

EXTERIOR. RAWALPINDI. EARLY EVENING.

We establish the city and its sounds as dusk approaches. At a distance, smoke can be seen rising and the sound of tear gas shells and bullets being fired.

Place and date flash on screen:

Pakistan, June 1977

Scene 2

EXTERIOR. RAWALPINDI STREET.

*As gas disperses we CU on helmeted policeman charging
demonstrators. Some of them are carrying the official poster-
picture of Bhutto with a large black cross throughout. Others
are carrying banners in Urdu and English:*

> Death to Bhutto.
>
> We want new elections.
>
> Bhutto! Why you cheated in elections?

*Most of the demonstrators are bearded, indicating their
Islamic loyalties. Police chase them away and they run,
dumping placards on the street. CU of placard on street with
Bhutto crossed out. Police feet run over it.*

Place flash:

> Rawalpindi

Scene 3

EXTERIOR. A RAWALPINDI BOULEVARD. DUSK.

Large ambassadorial limousine flying the Stars and Stripes is speeding down a large street. As it approaches a crossing it slows down. On the fringes, a small crowd with lots of cops. These are pro-Bhutto demonstrators. They are carrying the official poster-picture of the Leader. Placards:

Long live Bhutto,

Death to US imperialism, *etc.*

. . . As they see the car they charge down the road and surround it, chanting: 'Bhutto zindabad,' 'America kuttey, murdabad.'

Almost leisurely the police drag them away. Marked contrast to how they deal with anti-Bhutto men.

Scene 4

INTERIOR. AMBASSADORIAL CAR.

CU of Ambassador and wife in summer evening dress at the back of the car. Local chauffeur in uniform and Paul Turner, CIA Station Chief, next to him, in front. The couple is looking worried. A stone hits the front screen and everyone cowers. Then through the car, we see police moving them on. Car moves slowly and picks up speed.

AMBASSADOR (*wiping sweat off his face*). How long is this mess going to last? Intolerable.

Turner turns around, nods slightly and smiles reassuringly.

Scene 5

EXTERIOR. PM'S HOUSE. RAWALPINDI.

We establish the PM's house. The gate is surrounded by policemen who are armed, as well as plainclothes policemen. Cars are inspected carefully before they are let through.

Ambassadorial car reaches gates. It is stopped. Three cops peer in and smile. Plainclothes cop inspects car and chauffeur's window. He nods. Car drives in.

Scene 6

INTERIOR. PM'S HOUSE. RAWALPINDI. EVENING.

A buffet reception is in progress. Bhutto/Nusrat/Benazir are receiving guests. The room is half-full. Liveried servants are prancing about, offering drinks. From the corner of the room near the entrance, Bhutto's old family retainer, Hussein, is observing the ritual with a cynical expression on his weather-beaten face. An aide-de-camp is whispering names of new arrivals who are beginning to move around, to Bhutto. Most of the men are dressed in PPP uniforms. Their wives, in glamorous saris. Foreign diplomats are in evening gear.

ADC. The American Ambasador, sir.

US Ambassador and wife walk in. Followed by Paul Turner.

BHUTTO (*the mask is on*). Welcome, Your Excellency. Madame. (*Hands are shaken, then Bhutto stares hard at Turner.*) Glad you brought Mr Turner along. Nusrat. Benazir. Mr Turner. A very important man.

Turner shakes hands and forces a smile.

AMBASSADOR (*smiling*). Nice to see you again. We almost didn't make it. An angry mob, Prime Minister. Your supporters, I gather, were stoning us. (*Smiles again.*)

BHUTTO (*smiling as well*). I wonder why? Mr Turner

(*looking at him*) has been busy touring the country.
He knows the mood well, especially of our opposition. (*Laughs*) You better watch it, most people
think he's the real Prime Minister.

Polite frozen smiles. American party moves on.

*In the distance we can see General Zia arriving in full dress
uniform. He salutes Bhutto, who shakes his hands and pats
him on the back. Both men are engaged in an ultra-friendly
exchange. We see Bhutto laughing. In the background
Cherry and Lily are entering. The Bhutto women spy them
first and exchange looks. Nusrat moves off deliberately.
Benazir stays still. CU of Bhutto.*

BHUTTO. Hi, Bob.

Cherry grins and they shake hands.

BHUTTO (*cont'd*). You've met my daughter?

*Cherry nods and shakes hands with Benazir, who escorts him
to the nearest liveried servant and a whisky. Bhutto stares
hard at Lily. She smiles. They shake hands.*

BHUTTO (*releasing her hand slowly*). My dear Lily. I
heard you were in town. I'm not sure if I'm
pleased. You usually arrive at the beginning or
end of governments.

LILY (*smiling*). I'm very happy to see you again, Prime
Minister. (*Then, in a less formal tone as Nusrat frowns from
a distance*) But things are not so good . . . Hmm? Six

cites under Martial law. Six? *You* of all people bringing the uniforms back into play. Why?

Bhutto is pensive but does not reply. Instead, he beckons a waiter and they each take a glass.

Scene 7

EXTERIOR. DESERTED CANTONMENT ROAD. RAWALPINDI.
EVENING.

We establish a large nondescript bungalow. No other build-
ings in sight. Lone soldier stands guard with rifle on ready.
We see a car approaching. We catch a glimpse of General
Azad. His face is relaxed. Car enters gate as sentry presents
arms. Azad salutes back.

Scene 8

INTERIOR. MILY BUNGALOW, LARGE ROOM. EVENING

One of the special HQs utilized by military intelligence. A giant map of Pakistan on the wall. Six giant pins mark the cities where the Army is operating. Rectangular tables surrounded by chairs. Four Generals in the room. Two are inspecting the map. The Colonel and two other Generals are sitting at the table where teacups and saucers have been neatly laid out. Azad enters the room smiling. Seeing the assembled company his smile fades.

AZAD. Where's Chief General Zaman?

ZAMAN. He will be here soon. He's at PM's house but I have briefed him. We were waiting for you, General Azad!

All settle down.

ZAMAN (*cont'd*). General Nizami will report on the law and order situation in Karachi and Lahore. It's not good.

Azad snorts.

ZAMAN. General?

Azad ignores him, opens his briefcase and removes an elegant silver flask

AZAD. Orderly! Orderly!

Orderly enters the room and salaams.

AZAD *(cont'd)*. *Pani, burf aur glass. Jaldi!* It's a bit late for tea.

Zaman cannot conceal his contempt. Orderly returns with glasses and ice-bucket. Azad takes three, pours whisky. Takes one and offers others to Iftikhar and Nizami. Ifty takes one. Nizami is about to but sees Zaman glaring at him. Changes his mind and shakes his head sheepishly. Azad roars with laughter.

AZAD. Oh! Something must be up for *you* to refuse a drink.

Azad's face becomes serious, as if he has realized that this is no ordinary meeting. He stares at Zaman, who gives a smile-sneer.

Scene 9

INTERIOR. PM'S HOUSE. RAWALPINDI. EVENING.

Reception in progress. Gender segregation has taken place—women in one part of the room, men in another—with two exceptions: Benazir is talking to Paul Turner and Lily is trying to extract information from General Zia.

LILY. General Zia,. I am not questioning your loyalty. But there are others in the Army and everyone knows they're angry. Why should they use their soldiers to pull Mr Bhutto's chestnuts out of the fire?

ZIA. Miss Lily, you can take it from me. Our Army is loyal to the Constitution.

In another corner of the room.

BENAZIR (*roaring with laughter*). Mr Turner, my father believes that your government is destabilizing our government. Is it true? (*Turner smiles*) You must know. You're the CIA boss here. Aren't you?

TURNER. Miss Bhootow, I thought you wanted to be a diplomat. (*She laughs again.*) All these demonstrations and strikes against your father. You really think that we have the power to turn all that stuff on?

14

BENAZIR. You have the money.

In the distance we hear Bhutto in full sway. The two stop talking and move towards Bhutto's circle. Benazir and Lily are the only women.

Bhutto is surrounded by diplomatic guests, including Americans. He is in full flood and enjoying himself hugely.

BHUTTO. Nixon was always a shifty bastard. (*Mimics*)
'I'm an old friend of Pakistan, Mr Bhootow, but can't give you what you want right now.' Still, I preferred him to Lyndon Johnson. That cowboy behaved like a Punjabi. Used to play with his balls all the time. One thing to do it on your ranch. But when meeting Third World heads of state, a bit grotesque.

Laughter, except from American diplomats.

BHUTTO (*cont'd*). He treated us all like ranch hands. I remember when I was Foreign Minister. Our first military dictator, Ayub Khan, took me along on a state visit to Washington. Johnson came up to our leader's daughter. Dragged her off to the dance floor. That was bad enough. Then he pinched her bottom.

Laughter.

BHUTTO (*cont'd*). Afterwards she told her father. Field, Marshall's advice? 'Keep quiet. No scandals.' So you see, we Pakistanis have always had a special relationship with Washington!

Laughter although there are one or two people present who are clearly not amused. Lily scurries off but Bhutto sees her trying to leave and rushes to grab her as his audience scatters.

BHUTTO (*taking Lily by the arm*). You're not rushing off are you, Countess? I thought we could meet later.

LILY. My crew arrived today. I have to meet them, brief the director. (*Smiles*)

BHUTTO. We shall meet next week. Before the interview. Agreed?

Lily nods and exits. Hussein rushes up to Bhutto and whispers. Bhutto nods. The guests are departing. Bhutto and Nusrat are saying their farewells. Hussein walks to Benazir, who is talking to Turner again

HUSSEIN (*in loud whisper*). Your father said it's time to say goodbye to the other guests

TURNER (*smiling*). Nice meeting you. (*Shakes hands*) Goodbye.

BENAZIR. Goodbye.

Hussein escorts her out of the room and then returns to supervise clearing up. Bhutto is talking to Zia and we see both men leave the room.

Scene 10

INTERIOR. MILY BUNGALOW. EVENING

Nizami has just sat down. Sweat is pouring down his face. The others have unbuttoned their collars. The temperature, both actual and political, is heated. The room is not air-conditioned, unlike PM's house. Azad is in a rage.

AZAD. Of course the ruddy situation is bad. That's why we're keeping order in six cities. My point is that it is returning to normal. I think Bhutto will do a deal with the Opposition and agree to new elections. And you know something? He'll win again. So your plans (*staring at Zaman*) are shortsighted and foolish.

ZAMAN. Bhutto has failed. We are the only people who can run this country. Everything's going to the dogs in the last five years. It's a bloody mess. Only we can restore stability and foreign confidence. There will be no more investments here if he stays in power. He will try to do a deal with the Opposition but (*reaching into his top pocket and pulling out a letter*) here's a letter from one Opposition leader, Kasim Khan. Pleads with us to topple Bhutto. Make this country safe for decent people.

AZAD. For decent people in Washington. (*Taps his fingers on the table.*) Yes, yes, I know. Where is the Chief? Further discusson is pointless in his absence.

The two men stare at each other. Then Azad smiles and pours himself another whisky.

Scene 11

EXTERIOR. RAWALPINDI. SIDE STREET. EVENING.

The street itself is small, narrow and dusty but sounds of traffic on the nearby main road pollutes the ears. Incessant blowing of horns by cars, motorbikes and scooters, noises of vendors, etc. We see a scooter-rickshaw stopping in front of a modest, nondescript apartment. We see Lily and a female companion in the back. They alight and the female companion pays the rickshaw driver his fare. They wait until he revs up and departs. Then they look around. Satisfied, they walk away briskly down the street and we see them entering another apartment.

Scene 12

INTERIOR. SMALL APARTMENT. EVENING.

Front door opens into a small sitting room. As Lily and her guide enter, an elderly, bald, bespectacled man rises, grabs a walking stick and immediately goes out to a small open court-yard.

Scene 13

EXTERIOR. SMALL COURTYARD. EVENING.

Lily follows Habib into courtyard where there is a 'takht posh' with mattress, cushions, etc.

HABIB. Welcome, my dear. Welcome. (*Shakes hands warmly.*) Long time! (*Sighs*)

The woman of the house shyly brings soft drinks on a tray and retreats.

LILY (*stares at him in amazement*). Habib, old friend. *Comment ca va?* What happened to you? You look a wreck!

HABIB. I don't talk about myself. See what's happening to the country, Lily? (*Pauses suddenly*) It's a mess. The uniformwallahs—Sharks! Scent blood.

LILY. But he's still very popular.

HABIB. Yes. But with the wrong people.

Scene 14

INTERIOR. BHUTTO'S STUDY. EVENING.

Bhutto is seated in an armchair. Zia, on the sofa.

BHUTTO. I know you're in a hurry to go. Azad told me you had a Corps. Commanders' meeting tonight. What about?

ZIA (*slightly alarmed, but recovers very quickly*) Pure routine, sir. Routine.

BHUTTO. Hmm. Anyway. I intend to lift Martial Law from all the cities, withdraw troops to barracks within the next fortnight. We have begun very serious talks with the Opposition. The riots seem to be fading. No more dollars to pay for them, eh?

He chuckles. Zia grins obediently.

ZIA. That is good news, sir!

BHUTTO. Next week I would like to address all the Corps. Commanders and inform them of what we intend to do. OK?

ZIA. At our GHQ sir?

BHUTTO. No! Here. Why, is there a problem?

ZIA. Er. No sir, no problem, but . . .

BHUTTO. C'mon. C'mon. What is it?

ZIA. Situation is tense, sir. Some Generals might be worried.

BHUTTO. What about?

ZIA. Well, sir. When you first took over you invited Military and Air Force chiefs here and then you asked for their resignations on the spot.

Bhutto roars with laughter. Zia grins and tension is defused.

BHUTTO (*laughs*). And I was right!

ZIA. Of course, sir. As always. (*Grins*)

BHUTTO (*serious*). No. No. I'm not *always* right. Your loyalty is the best thanks I have. All your predecessors were Bonapartes. Skulking in the bushes. Always eyeing the throne. Waiting to pounce on the politicians. They never gave democracy a chance! Field Marshall Ayub, not a very profound man, used to tell us (*mimics*) 'Democracy can never flourish in a hot climate We need weather like England.' Heaven forbid.

Zia grimaces nervously, as if grinning.

ZIA. Times have changed sir.

Both men laugh.

Scene 15

EXTERIOR. COURTYARD. HABIB'S FRIEND'S HOUSE. EVENING.

Lily and Habib are sipping drinks.

LILY. If this is all true, he can't last long.

HABIB. I'm afraid not. You know, I . . . (*pause*) I don't want him to fall. Despite everything. (*Smiles*) Surrounded himself with sycophants, time-servers. 'I am the People's Party. These are all my creatures.' Well, these creatures rigged the elections three months ago against his advice. More loyal than the king. (*Angry*) And you know, Lily? He would have won them anyway. Might have lost some seats in the big towns but the bulk of the countryside was and still *is* with him. Now the Opposition have got him where it hurts but they're too weak to do anything. It's the Generals, I'm afraid. Once again. And this time it'll be nasty.

LILY. But why, Habib, why—?

HABIB (*sighs*). He promised the people the moon. Food, clothes and shelter for all. I remember telling the crowds on his behalf that our People's Government would build schools and hospitals for the poor in the large mansions of the rich. (*Smiles at the memory*) People believed us, Lily. He couldn't deliver. He could have, but it needed a revolution. Your papers called him our Fidel Castro but he wasn't. So, finally, he made a pact with the very politicians we defeated and destroyed. He lifted the people to the skies, then dropped them to the ground. Confiscated their aspirations.

LILY. Saint-Just . . . !

HABIB. Saint-Just—?

LILY. 'Those who make the revolution half-way dig their own graves.'

HABIB. Look around you. There's no one except the Army. But this time they won't die for him in the streets. That's changed. Vote for him? Yes. But die? Face bullets in their hearts? I'm not sure.

Scene 16

INTERIOR. PM'S HOUSE. BHUTTO'S STUDY. NIGHT.

Bhutto is lying on the sofa dressed in salwar and kurta. He is reading a file marked 'Top Secret.' Hussein is seated on the floor, massaging Bhutto's feet and legs. Hussein smiles. Bhutto puts the file on the floor, puts his hands behind his head and is deep in thought. He looks at his old servant and they exchange looks. This is the signal for Hussein to chat.

Scene 17

INTERIOR. MILY BUNGALOW. NIGHT.

The atmosphere is very tense. Zia is presiding over the meeting. The Generals have just finished reading a file marked 'Top Secret! Operation Wheeljam/Final Phase/All copies to be returned.' Azad and Iftikhar are manifestly livid. Zaman is cold and hard. Nizami uneasy. Zia alone is totally calm.

AZAD (*holding up document*). I don't accept this. I'm not convinced. This is a contingency plan, but the contingency is not there. (*Looking at Zia*) Is it, sir? (*Points to the map*) The cities are under control. Bhutto is in a mood to compromise. Why should we dirty our fingers in this mess? Leave it to the politicians.

ZIA. I tend to agree with you, but all that is being proposed is a takeover to provide breathing space. It will be a clean affair. No bloodshed. Elections within three months. Return to barracks.

Azad looks at him coldly.

ZIA (*cont'd*). You know me well. Am I hungry for power? We cannot afford a third Martial Law. But please General Azad, do understand the need for urgency. We are seeing a boxing match without a referee.

IFTIKHAR. But the match is nearly over and the boxers are about to agree to new rules. All this without a referee. I agree with General Azad. No reason to take over now.

ZAMAN (*cold*). Yes! Many reasons to strike *now*. Time is right. General Azad, you know who supplies our Army. Where we get the latest equipment? Who authorizes it?

AZAD. I know. I know.

ZAMAN. They are not pleased with the situation. They have put an embargo on military aid.

AZAD. Your Mecca is the Pentagon. Washington.

ZAMAN. I'm a realist.

AZAD. You talk of Islam, religion, patriotism. (*Gives a hollow laugh*) Sometimes I wonder whether our Army is meant to defend Pakistan or the United Islamic State of America.

ZIA. Please. No more. We'll meet again tomorrow.

Scene 18

EXTERIOR. A PRIVATE TENNIS COURT. RAWALPINDI. DAY.

Cherry and Paul Turner are finishing off a set. It is pre-breakfast time, before the sun is really hot. Both men are sweating profusely. An ace from Cherry finishes the set. Turner grins. Both men walk to two low armchairs on the side, serve themselves large glasses of fresh lime juice and water, add ice and sit down.

TURNER (*grinning again*). Your tennis is great, Bob, you're going to lose the big one here.

CHERRY (*tense*). I'm listening.

TURNER. Mr Bhootow's time is up. Everyone in Washington wants him out.

CHERRY (*sits up straight*). Everyone?

Turner nods.

CHERRY (*cont'd*). Pentagon?

Turner nods.

CHERRY (*cont'd*). CIA?

More nods.

CHERRY (*cont'd*). Defence Intelligence Agency?

Nod.

CHERRY (*cont'd*). The State Department?

Turner pauses, then nods. Cherry looks aghast.

TURNER. Check your sources, Bob, but it's true.

CHERRY. Why the fuck—?

Cherry is silenced by the news. He rises. Turner follows. They walk away.

TURNER (*cont'd*). Tell him to quit politics. He's finished here. He needs a long rest, preferably in Europe.

CHERRY. I can't believe it. And if he doesn't quit?

TURNER (*shrugs his shoulders*). Not our problem. The uniforms who take over will find a solution, I'm sure.

Both men walk into the house.

Scene 19

INTERIOR. SITTING ROOM IN PM'S HOUSE. DAY.

The room is formal but the PM is sprawled informally on the sofa. A relaxed atmosphere. Bhutto stares at Cherry thoughtfully. Then walks slowly to the end of the room, picks out a cigar, bites and chews it. Before he lights it, he turns sharply to Cherry.

BHUTTO. How sure are you?

CHERRY. My sources are reliable. You know that.

BHUTTO. Disinformation.

CHERRY. I know when I'm being used. Not this time.

BHUTTO. But why? Why?

CHERRY. Washington feels you're expendable.

BHUTTO (*laughing grimly*). Kissinger's curse!

Cherry looks at him, not understanding the reference.

BHUTTO (*cont'd*). 'If you don't give up your plans to build a nuclear reactor, we'll make a horrible example out of you.'

CHERRY. What did you say?

BHUTTO. I reminded him that we were an independent country. I was an elected leader accountable to my people, unlike himself.

CHERRY (*smiling*). Naughty. Third World leaders can't speak to us like that. It's not just him now. You've united them all . . . the CIA, the DIA, the Pentagon, the White House, even the State Department! An impressive achievement! They all want you out.

BHUTTO (*chuckling*). And I've united the Opposition parties as well. Unheard of! We have our cock-eyed Pathan from the frontier. Confused idiot. Loathes me. Of course. It's an obsession with him. (*He is now schoolboyish.*) Did you know his wife was caught stealing panties at Marks and Spencers in London?

Cherry shakes his head and laughs.

BHUTTO (*cont'd*). She was convicted. A fine. Her husband said it was an imperialist-Zionist plot! (*Both men laugh.*) She returned home red-faced. Denied it all. Frame up, etc., etc., . . . Then her husband's best friend, or so we thought, an upright old feudal type, also gave a press conference on the subject. (*Mimics*) 'Why should this decent lady steal panties in the first place. She never wears any.' Cherry? How did he know? Our workers and peasants demand an answer!

CHERRY (*smiling*). It's this side of you that they hate. Can I ask you something?

BHUTTO (*lighting a cigar*). Off the record?

CHERRY. Of course!

Bhutto nods.

CHERRY (*cont'd*). Why do you have to *humiliate* your opponents? Isn't defeating them enough? You treat dissenters as enemies. To be destroyed. Wiped off the map. Why?

Bhutto puffs away for a minute.

CHERRY (*cont'd*). I'm asking you this as a friend.

BHUTTO (*deadly serious*). I suppose it's the Sindhi landlord in me. We're a terribly primitive class of property owners, you know. Feudal. Let me shock you, Robert Cherry. I have, in time, exercised all my rights as a landlord. Yes, even the *droit de seigneur.*

Cherry is silent.

BHUTTO (*cont'd*). You haven't answered *my* question, Mr Robert Cherry. Who will the CIA put in my place? (*Stares hard at Cherry*) No riddles today, my friend.

CHERRY. No need for riddles. You know my countrymen. We believe the free world is best defended by military dictators

It sinks in. Bhutto is shocked, outraged. He pales, explodes.

BHUTTO. Impossible! I've removed every potential Bonaparte. Zia is my man! I shunted seven senior Generals to put him there!

Cherry looks directly at Bhutto.

BHUTTO (*cont'd*). A third round of military rule? Has Washington gone mad? Zia's a simpleton!

CHERRY. Listen, my friend. Zia may have been created by you but he belongs to the Army. This Army, like many others, is loyal first of all to those who keep it supplied. The Pentagon. And the Army offers the Pentagon stability.

BHUTTO. The Army! An Army can't exist without soldiers. Generals are like landlords and capitalists. They would be nowhere without their peasants and workers. And the soldiers like me. I had 90,000 of them released from Indian POW camps. Yes, *I* did that.

Scene 20

INTERIOR. ZIA'S OFFICE. MILY GHQ. DAY.

Azad is seated. Zia is at his most friendly. Both men are sipping cold drinks.

AZAD. In 1971 the Army was finished. Finished! If Bhutto had hanged 20 Generals in public, the people would have applauded.

ZIA. You think I don't know what Bhutto did for us? But it is no longer a private matter. Americans are very angry because of nuclear programme.

AZAD. *We* pressured Bhutto to start our own nuclear plans. Zaman said, 'Sir, we cannot sit back, while India tests nuclear devices.' So Bhutto told the world.

ZIA. Correct. But what worries the Pentagon very much is civilians controlling nuclear weapons. Unstable. Unstable. In Fort Bragg they made it very clear that even their president in the White House was not completely independent. He is always flanked by military advisors. General Barnes laughed and said to us: 'You see, we have a permanent semi-Martial Law in *our* country. No one objects.'

AZAD. Cheeky bastard. Do you know, sir, I was hijacked

by Colonel Shepherd, the Military Attaché at their bloody embassy. We drove around in his car for one hour. Against my will. You know what he said? 'Why are you resisting Zia, General Azad. Your country's future is at stake. Can't you see what's going on?'

Zia appears shocked.

AZAD (*cont'd*). I told the bugger I'm a serving General in the *Pakistan* Army. I don't talk politics with foreigners. He laughed. Called me naive. What shocked me was that he knew everything. All our top secret discussions. Why?

Zia and Azad stare at each other. Azad angry. Zia shifty. As Azad gets up to leave, Zia rises too and puts his hand on Azad's shoulder.

ZIA. Military security is paramount. Always!

AZAD. Sir?

ZIA. I know you like Bhutto, I like him too. But please don't make the mistake of telling him about our conversations.

Azad appears shocked.

ZIA (*cont'd*). I know the temptation, but *he* won't like you for it. He might think we've sent you.

Scene 21

EXTERIOR. LAWN. PM'S HOUSE. DAY.

BHUTTO. No, no, Bob. Zia is not that clever. If there's a coup, they'll push him aside. I've kept him flanked with three, er . . . I suppose you could call them democratic Generals. Iftikhar, Rehman, but above all Azad. They won't overthrow democratic governments.

CHERRY. Even democratic Generals want a united Army. It's their only power base. Without it they are nothing. (*Rises*) They're going to jam your wheels hard, my friend.

The only reply is a puff of smoke from Bhutto's cigar. Cherry turns to leave. Then he pauses. Turns around. Stands behind Bhutto and presses his shoulders affectionately.

CHERRY. You take care now

BHUTTO. Don't worry, Bob. I won't let them make a Charley out of me. And Bob!

Cherry pauses near the door and turns around.

BHUTTO (*cont'd*). Thanks (*waving him away*).

Scene 22

INTERIOR. BHUTTO'S STUDY. DAY.

Zia is seated on the armchair, smoking. Bhutto enters from a side door. Zia stands to attention, puts out his cigarette behind his back and throws it on the carpet. Bhutto stares at him coldly. The atmosphere is in sharp contrast to the previous meeting. Bhutto sits behind his desk, stressing the formality of the occasion. He keeps Zia standing for a moment while he signs a few papers.

BHUTTO. Please sit down, General Zia (*indicating chair on other side of the desk*).

ZIA (*a picture of humility*). Sir?

BHUTTO How did your meeting go yesterday?

ZIA (*taken aback, but recovers*). Pure routine.

Bhutto stares at him. Contempt is written on his face.

BHUTTO. *Pure* routine?

ZIA. Yes, sir.

BHUTTO. Hmm. General, what is your assessment of the political crisis?

ZIA. Sir?

BHUTTO (*slowly, as if talking to a dimwit*). Let me simplify. How do you read the present situation?

38

Zia nervous. Grins, then ultra-humble.

BHUTTO. Nothing is impossible in politics.

ZIA. Any orders for us, sir?

BHUTTO (*staring hard*). Yes! I order the Army not to interfere in politics. I can still save this country. Don't point your tanks at me.

ZIA. God forbid, sir. God forbid.

Scene 23

EXTERIOR. PM'S HOUSE. DAY.

Ministerial cars disgorge Cabinet Ministers. Soldiers salute them as they enter PM's house.

Scene 24

INTERIOR. CABINET ROOM IN PM'S SECRETARIAT. DAY.

Two large air conditioners are pumping in cold air. A large, rectangular table with a green top is surrounded by upright, upholstered chairs. There are two portraits in the room; the larger one, above an ornamental mantelpiece, is Jinnah's and the smaller, on an opposite wall, is Bhutto's. A vase containing wilting flowers adorns the table at the head of which is the PM's swivel chair. Two peons are providing the finishing touches: cups and saucers are being laid on the table as well as tumblers. Suddenly the door opens and the Cabinet Ministers enter the room. The peons salaam and withdraw. Ministers take their seats to the right and left of the PM. They are all attired in the Party's summer uniform—white trousers with a red stripe and matching tunic. As they take their seats we flash the date across the screen:

29th June, 1977

Bhutto enters, flanked by Rashid, his political assistant. All rise.

BHUTTO. Please sit.

All sit.

BHUTTO *(cont'd)*. Only one item for discussion today.
The situation is approaching a point of no return.
Rashid will brief you on the latest developments.

Rashid settles his papers and stands up.

RASHID. We have decided to convene the new National Assembly, despite Opposition boycott. The time has come to take the offensive.

BHUTTO (*sipping water*). Forget the Opposition boycott, we have to convince them that our offer of an election is genuine. Elections throughout the country and without any preconditions by either side.

Akbar excited just like everyone else since Bhutto's statement is a complete volte-face.

AKBAR (*looking straight at Bhutto*). There's one problem, Zulfy.

The look on the Bhutto's face conveys that Akbar has overstepped the mark. Akbar is about to apologize.

BHUTTO (*cold anger*). Don't you Zulfy me just because I've fucked your wife.

Silence. Bhutto sips some water.

BHUTTO (*cont'd*). Carry on.

AKBAR (*paralysed with shame, stuttering*). Er, er, it was nothing, sir. I'm sorry.

Stunned silence.

WHISKEY. Sirrr.

Bhutto looks at him.

WHISKEY (*cont'd*). With great respect, sirr, er, er . . .

BHUTTO. What is it? Speak up.

WHISKEY. I talk to lots of ordinary people, sirr. Poor
people, like myself. Your supporters, sirr.

*Bhutto raises his eyebrows, gestures with his hand to speed
Whiskey up. Whiskey sweats profusely, is nervous and shifty,
does not look at Bhutto while talking but at a blank wall.*

WHISKEY (*cont'd*). Our supporters want us to stand firm,
sirr. They don't want to give too much concessions
to reactionaries and traitors. Sirr, we can't release
Baluch rebels. They have waged war against our
government, our Army and . . .

BHUTTO (*interrupts angrily*). Ordinary people? Poor citi-
zens? Where are you talking about? The pimps
who share your whisky or the whores who share
your bed in that filthy hotel you patronize?

*Whiskey's hands have started trembling. He attempts to gulp
down some water.*

Scene 25

INTERIOR. MILY BUNGALOW. NIGHT.

The six Generals are seated around the same table. They have been talking for some time.

AZAD. We must treat Bhutto like any other politician. That's what we agreed yesterday. If he wins, he can be Prime Minister again.

Zaman and Nizami can barely contain themselves. Zia is impassive.

ZAMAN (*to Zia*). Sir, will you make Azad see sense? If Bhutto were returned to power . . . (*shakes his head in despair*). Disaster! He is not a generous man. We would be tried for treason and shot.

AZAD. And what do you propose?

ZAMAN. Despatch him when we take over. Like that Allende (*pronounced Allendy*) in Chile. We say he opened fire on us. His supporters will be happy he died a martyr.

AZAD (*on his feet*). Outrageous! (*Stares with hatred at Zaman*) I still command the Armoured Division. My men will not accept cold-blooded murder.

ZAMAN. General Azad. I get daily Intelligence reports. Yes, he is unpopular today. But out of power he will lie, make excuses, blame others for his crimes. Many who curse him today will cheer him tomorrow. Then he will chop our heads off. Including yours, General. He must be despatched without delay.

All are silent for a few seconds. Everyone stares at Zia.

ZIA. I veto the plan. No shooting.

ZAMAN (*coldly*). You will regret this decision.

Scene 26

INTERIOR. PM'S DINING ROOM. NIGHT.

The room is ornate. Richly carpeted, with a chandelier and expensive furniture. Persian rugs and a tiger skin cover the carpet. On the mantelpiece and tables there are photographs of Bhutto with various world leaders: Nixon, Mao, Brezhnev, Indira Gandhi. An attractive Hungaro-Italian woman is eyeing the artefacts and sipping whisky from an expensive cut-glass tumbler. It is Lily. She turns as the door opens and Bhutto walks in. They shake hands warmly.

BHUTTO. Nice to see you alone.

LILY. This time I wanted the interview

Bhutto pours himself a small whisky.

BHUTTO. I know who you've been seeing, Lily. My enemies. Yesterday's men. (*Mutters*) Senile old fool.

LILY. Your friend Mr Cherry tells me that the rulers of our free world are determined. Bhutto must go, they say . . . (*looks at him*).

BHUTTO. Cherry forgets my trump card.

LILY. I'm waiting . . .

BHUTTO. The people. My people harken to me. If I call them out on the streets . . .

There is a knock on the door and Hussein enters. He smiles knowingly at Lily who blushes, then walks straight up to Bhutto.

HUSSEIN. The Generals are waiting.

Bhutto looks at his watch, nods to Lily.

LILY. Till tomorrow?

Bhutto walks out briskly.

LILY (*to Hussein*). I'm worried about him, you know. The Army is not under his control.

Hussein smiles but does not say anything. He is waiting to show her out. She finishes her drink and leaves, followed by him.

Scene 27

INTERIOR. PM'S STUDY. NIGHT.

A spectacled Bhutto is sitting at his desk. Zia and Zaman are standing to attention. Bhutto deliberately keeps them standing. Finally, he looks up.

BHUTTO. Please sit down.

Zia and Zaman take their seats opposite him.

BHUTTO (*cont'd*). I thought I had requested a meeting with all the Corps. Commanders.

ZIA (*clearing his throat*). They had other tasks today, sir.

BHUTTO (*to Zaman*). Nice you could fine the time.

ZAMAN (*deadpan*). Always a pleasure to hear you directly, sir.

BHUTTO. I haven't much time. Parliament is waiting. Please inform the High Command that I intend to accept all Opposition demands. Cabinet has endorsed this decision. We'll have new elections within three months. You look worried, General Zaman. You should be happy. Troops back in barracks. End of street violence. Peace everywhere. (*Pauses, lights a cigar.*) Or is it that you're worried I might win again? (*Chuckles*) You can go, gentlemen. (*They rise*) One more thing. (*Coldly*) Your soldiers shot an innocent smallholder in Karachi yesterday.

ZAMAN. He breached the curfew, sir.

BHUTTO. Curfew! Curfew! The poor don't know what the word means. That man was alone with his pathetic barrowcart. Your officers killed him. A hundred thousand people marched behind his body today. A hundred thousand. The poor of Karachi. My supporters, General. Don't be in a rush to kill them.

ZIA. I will report your view to the High Command, sir.

Scene 28

INTERIOR. NATIONAL ASSEMBLY CHAMBER. NIGHT.

One side is full. Opposition benches are empty. Crowded government benches, lacklustre. Lots of yawning and stretching. Neon lights fail to dispel the gloom. There are armed policemen in the Chamber. The Diplomat's Gallery is packed with white and black and a few Chinese faces. In the Visitor's Gallery we see General Zaman and two unidentified Intelligence officers. In the Press Gallery we see Cherry, Lily and others. Cherry and Lily are chatting animatedly. The front bench is occupied by the Cabinet with Khalid and Akbar next to Bhutto's empty seat and Whiskey at the other end.

Whiskey is slightly tipsy. As a large wall clock strikes midnight, Bhutto enters, dressed immaculately in a summer suit. Whisky rises to his feet and starts applauding wildly. Others applaud more sedately. Bhutto smiles at Khalid and takes his seat, providing a cue for the Speaker.

SPEAKER. Honourable members, I welcome you to this special session of Parliament. I am sad that our Opposition parties have decided to boycott this session. It reminds me of what our greatest poet, Iqbal, once said . . .

At this point he catches Bhutto's eye. The leader signals his impatience.

SPEAKER (*cont'd*). I call on the Prime Minister, Mr
Zulfikar Ali Bhutto, to address this house.

BHUTTO (*rises slowly and moves to despatch box*). Mr
Speaker, honourable members. We are at the political crossroads once again. Our country still bleeding from the wounds of the last war with India, still
suffering from the pangs of enforced separation
from East Pakistan, now Bangladesh, is being
threatened again. For five years this government
has tried to build a new Pakistan. Our vision was of
a country whose social standards could become
comparable to parts of Europe. We wanted, and
still want, a society engaged in a permanent war
against illiteracy and ignorance, prejudice and
obscurantism. A society in which men and women
are equals. We have sought to mobilize the collective energies of our people, to give them education
and medical aid, to clean the towns, to improve
the villages, give every citizen a dignity that is his
due. Of course, we haven't achieved this. We
always knew it would be a long haul. They always
do. The scale of their violence forced us to use the
Army to restore law and order. The crisis we con-
front now is serious. Very serious. We could resolve
it tomorrow, or this very night, if the actors were
all indigenous.

Pauses. Pindrop silence. Now his tone changes from a reflective statesman to a more fiery and passionate form of oratory.

BHUTTO (*cont'd*). But I am angry tonight. Because I know that foreign powers are destabilizing our country. They never learn. They carry on as before.

Cries of 'name them, name them.'

BHUTTO (*cont'd*). You know who they are. So does the Opposition. They are the ones who use their currency.

CHERRY (*whispers to Lily*). Beginning of the end.

Lily nods sadly.

BHUTTO. The Oppostion is playing with fire. They appeal to the Generals to intervene. There are meetings at the American Embassy here in Teheran. They dig out old contingency plans and prepare to perpetrate misdeeds against our people.

Cries of 'shame, shame.'

BHUTTO (*cont'd*). Yes, it is a cause for shame that people who are supposed to protect our country, defend our borders, are talking to foreign ambassadors. It is an intolerable form of interference in our internal affairs. (*Looking at the Gallery*) Don't treat *us* as one of your Banana Republics. The bloodhounds are on my trail. After my blood. They killed

President Allende in Chile, inaugurating a regime of terror and torture, but they could not do the same in Vietnam.

Loud applause.

CHERRY (*to Lily*). He's committing suicide.

Some diplomats walk out, followed by Zaman and his aides. Other diplomats are laughing at Bhutto.

BHUTTO. The source of our power is invincible. The people. My people harken to me. *They* are my strength, my iron will, my determination, my conscience. We owe them everything. Without them we are nothing. Nothing. With them we cannot be defeated. Never!

There is a prolonged applause. Shouts of 'Long Live Chairman Bhutto.' The faithful have now woken up and are enthused. Silence.

BHUTTO (*cont'd*). I want to tell you something

Bhutto pauses. Everyone waits. Expectant hush. Slowly, he takes out of his pocket a two-paged typed letter and holds it up for all to see.

CHERRY (*quietly*). Don't do it, my friend.

LILY (*transfixed by Bhutto*). Too late, Bob. The die is cast.

BHUTTO. This is a letter from Mr Cyrus Vance, the American Secretary of State. He has the nerve to write to me and suggest a meeting between us to resolve the political crisis in Pakistan. As if we were a pliant satrapy. *He* could solve *our* crisis!

Shocked gasps.

BHUTTO (*cont'd*). He wants to act on behalf of the Opposition, the *Pakistan National Alliance*. My answer to Vance is simple. *No!*

Prolonged applause.

BHUTTO (*cont'd*). I refuse to barter the sovereignity of my country in this fashion. (*Looking up at the Gallery*) Find someone else to do your dirty work. The party isn't over.

Scene 29

EXTERIOR. GOVERNMENT BUILDINGS. ISLAMABAD. DAY.

Zia and Zaman walk through the courtyard, down steps and through another courtyard. Occasionally nodding and smiling at government officers as they walk by.

ZAMAN. The way he talks now. I'm sure he knows.

ZIA (*grins reassuringly*). He suspects. He does not know.

ZAMAN. But his speech to the Assembly . . .

ZIA. Hot air. He's concerned. That much he knows. No more.

ZAMAN. The attack on the Americans was strong. Too hard. He's never gone so far before.

ZIA (*grinning*). Nor have the Americans.

ZAMAN. Sir, you underestimate him.

ZIA. I don't think so.

ZAMAN. We should despatch him.

ZIA No!

ZAMAN. No accidents?

ZIA. No. There are dangers. If the people come out for Bhutto, it could get messy.

ZAMAN. If the people come out it means civil war. The Army will not hold. Many soldiers will not open fire. Azad knows that well.

ZIA. Exactly. Question: will they come out? Perhaps if
Bhutto were to appeal to them directly. But Bhutto
will not do that. He is relying on a deal with the
Opposition leaders. And he is not sure if the people will come out for him.

ZAMAN. If they did, it might go too far.

ZIA. He knows that well. So he will manoeuvre. Not call
the people out. And in the ways of manoeuvre, we
have more training.

ZIA (*cont'd*). No, the real danger is above. Air Force. Air
Force chiefs like Bhutto. We have not involved
them in *Operation Wheeljam*. Suppose they get wind
of our plans. Bomb our tanks. Take Bhutto in safety
to Air Force base. That must be avoided.

ZAMAN. Air Force strike? That's just impossible, sir.

ZIA (*quietly*). That's very possible.

Scene 30

INTERIOR. CABINET ROOM. NIGHT.

The door slowly opens. Whiskey creeps in and takes his seat.
Bhutto carries on talking, completely ignoring the late
entrant. No one else looks at him. A Cabinet meeting in
progress. We peer in from the window and watch a tableau.

Scene 31

EXTERIOR. ROAD. DAY.

Zia in his military limousine speeding to Military Intelligence HQ.

Scene 32

INTERIOR. MILITARY HQ. DAY.

All five Generals are present. Zia strides in, goes straight to the head of the table.

ZIA (*serious, tense*). Generals, we are now short of time. We must strike tonight. *Operation Wheeljam* at Zero Hour.

AZAD. What the hell is going on? I've just returned from Lahore. The city is calm.

IFTIKHAR. And I hear Bhutto's done a deal with the Opposition.

ZIA. Exactly. You know the basis? All the Baluch gangsters are to be released now or just before elections. Do you realize the effect this will have? It will legitimize rebellion. These men waged war against our state. To release them is an intolerable provocation.

AZAD. I take the point, but to launch a coup—an over-reaction, sir! I cannot be party to a move that is *seen* as a blatant violation of democracy.

ZAMAN. They will say we're preventing the politicians from reaching an agreement.

ZIA. Our country's integrity is now at stake. It is now

our duty as guardians of this Islamic Republic to preserve our religion and our country. That's why Pakistan exists. We are like Israel. An ideological state. Take Judaism out of Israel and it will collapse. Take Islam out of Pakistan and make it a secular state and we will collapse. The Pakistan Army *is* Pakistan.

AZAD. Now I see it all. The mullahs have got you in their grip. Remember Black September in Jordan? Did you think about Islam when you helped King Hussein butcher the Palestinians?

ZAMAN. Shut your mouth. He is our chief.

ZIA (*calm*). Do you know that Bhutto has got Cabinet approval to sack us all tomorrow?

Azad, Ifty and Rahman are clearly shocked.

AZAD. Where is the proof?

ZAMAN (*rises, walks to the door and shouts*). Bring him in, Colonel

Azad and the others are amazed as the Colonel enters with Whiskey, looking extremely cocky in contrast to Cabinet appearances.

ZIA. Here, my dear General Azad, is the proof. Straight from a Cabinet meeting.

AZAD. So I see. Is it sober? (*To Whiskey*) Is all this I hear true, you rogue?

WHISKEY. General-sahib, would I risk my life to come
here and inform you otherwise? These two ears
heard Bhutto. These two eyes read the papers
ordering all your dismissals. Rashid, that bastard,
said you should be executed for treason. All of you
will spend tomorrow night in prison.

*Azad stares at him hard. He is shattered. He turns away from
Whiskey in disgust and indicates that the man be removed.
No one moves.*

AZAD (*angry*). Get him out of here. The stench is
unbearable.

Zia nods to Colonel who exits with Whiskey.

AZAD. So Bhutto found out about us. I should have
known. We are plotting. He is right to try and get
rid of us. (*To Zaman*) You've trapped me.

Zaman shrugs.

ZIA. Now are you convinced?

Azad doesn't reply.

ZIA (*signals to everyone to sit*). At Zero Hour we imple-
ment *Operation Wheeljam*. Zaman and I will take
Bhutto. Nizami will supervise mopping-up opera-
tions. The whole Cabinet and heads of Police and
Security to be dealt with before we take him. All
communications to and from Bhutto's house to be
cut off at midnight. Rahman, you fly to Quetta and

take over that province. Iftikhar, you become the
Frontier. Nizami will take the Punjab. Zaman and I
will keep here.

AZAD. And me? Ambassador to Austria?

ZIA (*smiling*). General Azad, you are too important to
waste on administering provinces. You must stay in
command of the Armoured Corps. We can't take
everyone out of the Army.

All rise.

ZIA (*cont'd*). Just one more thing. If Bhutto summons
any of you to his house today, don't go!

All laugh except Azad.

Scene 33

EXTERIOR. STREETS OF RAWALPINDI. NIGHT.

We see a courtyard full of empty trucks. Suddenly soldiers enter from different directions in full battle gear and pile into the trucks which then drive out of the courtyard in a convoy. At one point, the convoy breaks up into two. Soldiers leap out of the trucks, barricade the street and take up positions. A jeep draws up. The Colonel jumps out, hurries to the barricade, inspects it, nods his approval, then jumps back in and drives on until he overtakes the rest of the convoy. Elsewhere, soldiers are clearing bystanders and stragglers off the street. We hear murmurs of 'Why?' 'Manoeuvres!' etc. Street lights begin to go out. As the action is continuing, a time and date flash across the screen:

4th July, 1977. 9.45 p.m.

Scene 34

EXTERIOR. PM'S HOUSE. NIGHT.

We first hear the sounds of lorries and jeeps on the streets and then their shadowy silhouettes can be seen. Jeeps and armoured cars are moving in different directions. They surround the PM's house. Not far away shadowy soldiers have erected barricades to take care of all eventualities. We hear a message being sent to GHQ.

SOLDIER'S VOICE. Tanks and soldiers in place. The Leopard is surrounded. Repeat. The Leopard is surrounded.

RADIO VOICE. Message received. Congratulations!

Scene 35

EXTERIOR. PM'S HOUSE. LAWNS. NIGHT.

A man half-crawls, half-runs, camouflaging himself all the while, towards the house. He reaches the window of the pantry. From outside we can see the figure of Hussein. The guard knocks on the window. It opens.

GUARD. Brother Hussein! Brother Hussein!

The old servant sticks his head out of the window

HUSSEIN. What's going on

GUARD. Tell Bhutto-saab the tanks are moving in.
Army's surrounded all the neighbourng streets.
I'm sure they're coming here. Be careful. Please.
Be careful. Army man said he'd kill me if I left my post.

HUSSEIN. Get back, quick. Bless you, my son! (*Shuts window.*)

Scene 36

INTERIOR. DINING ROOM. NIGHT.

Bhutto is puffing a cigar and sipping brandy. He is relaxed in an armchair, his feet on a stool. Nusrat is sitting, her feet up on a sofa. Suddenly, the door bursts open and Hussein rushes in. The couple look at the old man in amazement.

NUSRAT. Are you OK? The children? What happened?

HUSSEIN. Tanks! Tanks! They're coming. One of the guards risked his life to tell us.

Bhutto leaps out of his chair.

BHUTTO. The bastards! Nusrat, wake up Benazir!

He rushes out and up the stairs to his study.

Scene 37

EXTERIOR. MILITARY HQ. NIGHT.

*Zia (followed by Colonel) and Zaman, wearing combat berets
and surrounded by an Army Unit with automatic weapons,
come down the steps of GHQ. A great deal of military hustle
and bustle in the courtyard with Army trucks and jeeps waiting and ready. As Zia comes down, he is saluted by soldiers
and cheered by junior officers. Zia and Zaman get into two
different jeeps. Zaman's is behind Zia's. They zoom off. In the
back of the jeeps are the armed men. We track the jeeps speeding out of the GHQ compound and onto the streets, which are
now deserted.*

Scene 38

EXTERIOR. STREET. NIGHT.

Zia and Zaman's jeeps come round the corner and are stopped at the barricade. The Major in command recognizes Zia and salutes.

ZIA. Well done, Major. No trouble?

MAJOR (*saluting with a broad smile*). No sir!

ZIA (*to Zaman over his roofless jeep, loudly, sounding louder in the still of night*). General Zaman, the Leopard is in the bag. *Operation Wheeljam* is over. Radio the news to all Corps. Commanders.

ZAMAN. Yes, sir.

Jeeps speed on to PM's house.

Scene 39

INTERIOR. BHUTTO'S STUDY. NIGHT.

Bhutto holds the telephone receiver.

BHUTTO. Get me Zia! What! What! When?

Slams down the receiver as Nusrat enters the room. He looks at her.

BHUTTO (*cont'd*). They've cut us off. No communications. The house is surrounded.

Nusrat moves closer and hugs him.

Scene 40

INTERIOR. PM'S HOUSE. NIGHT.

*Two roofless jeeploads of officers and soldiers with machine
guns speed to the front of the bungalow. They are followed by
a third jeep being driven to Bhutto. The jeeps rendezvous at
the front door. Soldiers are everywhere. Zaman salutes Zia,
who returns the greeting. Both men, followed by armed soldiers, walk up the front stairs to the door.*

Scene 41

INTERIOR. BHUTTO'S STUDY. NIGHT.

Bhutto is standing, Benazir at his side. Nusrat is seated on the armchair, but on its edge. Hussein stands near the door, with his hands behind his back. In one of these, there is a revolver. Nusrat is pale with anxiety and scared.

BHUTTO. I will not tolerate any nonsense now. I want both of you to go to your bedrooms. Start packing. Hussein, I know what you're holding. Put that away. We don't want to give them any excuses. Don't forget they can kill on sight.

BENAZIR (*clutching her father's hand*). Please, papa! Please!

NUSRAT. The presence of women might be better. Restrain them. They won't kill us! (*In a different tone*) Will they?

BHUTTO. They want me. Not you. Let's not offer them any more targets. (*Kisses Benazir on her head*) Go child. Go. Hussein, take her to her room.

Benazir hugs him and leaves, followed by Hussein.

BHUTTO (*cont'd*). Don't think I don't know the dangers. These bastards could kill me. Then say I was resisting arrest. If they do, it is vital you're alive to tell the truth. If you're here they might . . . Oh, Nusrat.

The couple embrace.

NUSRAT. It can't end like this. It can't.

Outside, the noise of jeeps entering the compound can be heard. He frees himself from Nusrat's embrace.

BHUTTO. Hard times have begun again.

He walks her to the door and pushes her out gently. We catch a glimpse of her agonized face.

Scene 42

INTERIOR. PM'S HOUSE. NIGHT.

Zia, Colonel, Zaman and soldiers stride up the stairs to the door of the study. Zia halts, then deliberately knocks.

Scene 43

INTERIOR. BHUTTO'S STUDY. NIGHT.

Bhutto is in a cold rage.

BHUTTO (*barks*). Come in!

Zia, Zaman and Colonel enter. Zia salutes Bhutto.

BHUTTO (*cont'd*). You traitor. You pledged your loyalty to the Constitution. You snake, what do you think you're up to?

ZIA. Sorry, sir. Circumstances compelled us to act.

BHUTTO. Circumstances! Compelled! The Opposition had agreed to deal with us! You acted to prevent civilian politics from proceeding. You have stopped the constitutional processes of this country. You are traitors. Guilty of treason.

ZIA. We have only taken over to ensure a free and impartial election, sir. Within 90 days there will be an elected government again. I'll be saluting you again as Prime Minister.

BHUTTO. I still am Prime Minister. The only one ever to be elected in our entire history. Ninety days! Joke! Do you think the people will tolerate you that long?

ZAMAN (*moving forward*). You were the Prime Minister. Martial Law is now in force. Please get ready to leave this house.

Zaman opens the door. Soldiers pour in. Colonel takes Bhutto's arm. Bhutto gives Zia a hard stare. Then he is led out of the room followed by soldiers.

Scene 44

INTERIOR. LANDING OF PM'S HOUSE. NIGHT.

Benazir and Nusrat stand close to each other. Bhutto is led downstairs followed by soldiers and Generals.

NUSRAT (*frightened*). Excuse me, General Zaman.

Zaman pauses.

NUSRAT (*cont'd*). Where are you taking us?

ZAMAN. Government House in Murree. Protective custody. All of you will be together.

Scene 45

INTERIOR. TV STUDIO. DAY.

Announcers are waiting nervously. Zia arrives, surrounded by armed military guards. He senses nervousness and reassures the announcer, a woman.

ZIA. Nothing to worry about. Go ahead.

ANNOUNCER *(VO).* Assalam-aleikum. The time is 7 a.m. We have a special announcement. The country is now under Martial Law. We are taking you to the Military GHQ where the Chief Martial Law Administrator, General Zia-ul-Haq, is ready to broadcast to the nation.

Zia sits at his desk and begins his speech to the nation.

ZIA. My fellow countrymen, assalam-aleikum. The country is now under Martial Law. Our operation code-named *Fairplay* was carried out smoothly. Our aim is to create the best conditions for a return to democracy. It must be quite clear to you that when the political leaders failed to steer the country out of crisis, it would have been an inexcusable sin for the Armed Forces to sit as silent spectators. We saw no prospects of a compromise between government and Opposition. The country was on the

verge of chaos. We could not take the risk of stay-
ing aloof from politics. I want to make it absolutely
clear that neither I nor the Army have any political ambitions. My sole aim is to organize free and
fair elections within 90 days. I give a solemn assur-
ance that I will not deviate from this schedule.

Scene 46

EXTERIOR. RAWALPINDI. DAY.

A daytime shot of Rawalpindi similar to the one at the beginning of the film. Time flashes across screen:

Four Weeks Later

We see a large limousine, flying the Pakistan flag, negotiating the streets. We see Zia in the back of the car. The car drives into the courtyard of Military GHQ as soldiers at the gate present arms. Zia smiles and returns their salute. His every motion is beginning to exude power. The car stops. Colonel, seated in front of the car, jumps out and opens the door. More soldiers salute as Zia enters the building.

Scene 47

INTERIOR. MILITARY GHQ. ISLAMABAD. DAY.

*6th August, 1977. Zaman, Nizami, Iftikhar and Rahman
are seated around a table. Azad is absent. Zaman is staring
at an Urdu newspaper which shows a full-page picture of
Bhutto's triumph. He takes a fruit knife and gently, half
absentmindedly, sticks it through Bhutto's head in the picture.
Zia walks in. They stand. He sits. They sit.*

NIZAMI. We should never have released him!

ZAMAN (*cold and angry*). It was predictable. Too predictable. (*Pause. Flicks through paper. To Zia*) Have
you read it, sir?

Zia shakes his head, negatively.

ZAMAN (*cont'd*). You should. Same rhetoric. (*Reads*) 'We
are human beings, all of us. We all make mistakes.
Only God is infallible. But my mistakes were for
you. That's what they can't forgive. What am I
without you? A nobody. Nothing. That is why I am
here before you.' Yes, it is the same Bhutto . . . and
so on, sir. It's a clever speech.

ZIA. How can they forget! A month ago there were hundreds of delegations from Lahore. 'Our daughters
cannot walk the streets. Bhutto's goondas are
attacking them.' (*Grins*) Are the figures accurate?

IFTIKHAR. I was at the airport when his plane landed. Red, green and black flags everywhere. A sea of people. Amazing sight, sir. A quarter of a million there, at least.

RAHMAN. We must postpone the elections sir. Ninety days are not enough to defeat him.

Zia doesn't reply.

RAHMAN (*cont'd*). The longer we leave it, the more popular he gets.

NIZAMI. Elections? What elections?

Rahman and Iftikhar look at each other.

ZAMAN. Elections? (*He laughs*) That's no longer our problem. We can't leave him loose, sir. (*Looks at Zia.*)

ZIA (*stroking his moustache absentmindedly*). What do you suggest, General Zaman?

Scene 48

INTERIOR. LAHORE, LIVING ROOM. DAY.

Same day. Living room in a modest house. Sharp contrast to the finery of PM's house. No air conditioning, but slightly darkened room with cool floor, low chairs and cushions and durrees on the floor. Jugs of cold water on a side table, Akbar and Khalid are standing, chatting with a white-haired man who is sitting on the floor in the corner, gently smoking a cigarette. Khalid and Akbar are excited. The loss of power has made them human again. They are talking non-stop. Their clothes are salwar and kameez, slightly dirty and dusty. They are wiping the sweat off their faces at regular intervals. The ceiling fan can't keep them cool.

KHALID. I told you. Didn't I tell you? (*Laughs*) Couldn't even see the end of the crowd. Party flags everywhere. Everywhere. When the Boss stepped out the slogans could be heard all over the city.

As he is talking, chants are heard in the background, getting louder as they approach the house. 'Bhutto, Bhutto, Bhutto. Long Live our Bhutto. Long Live our Bhutto.'

Scene 49

EXTERIOR. MODEST BUNGALOW IN LAHORE. DAY.

Bhutto is getting out of a small car. Outside, a crowd waits, chanting and extending its hands. An old woman walks to him and kisses his hand. Bhutto gives her a hug.

Scene 50

INTERIOR. LIVING ROOM IN MODEST BUNGALOW, LAHORE.
DAY.

Bhutto enters, dressed in salwar and kameez. Dishevelled, with dust on his face. He is exultant. His face is not tired. An elderly man rises, walks to the table, wets a towel with ice-cold water and walks to Bhutto, cleans his face. Bhutto looks at him, his eyes fill with tears and he hugs him. For once, Bhutto is too moved to speak.

Scene 51

EXTERIOR. BUNGALOW IN LAHORE.

Cherry pushes his way through the excited crowd.

Scene 52

INTERIOR. LIVING ROOM, BUNGALOW IN LAHORE. DAY.

Bhutto sits, looking overwhelmed. The door opens. Enter Cherry, dusty and tired like the rest. He is wearing khaki trousers and a grey bush shirt. Bhutto looks at him and smiles though his tone reverts somewhat to the old Bhutto, as if for Cherry he still has to act Prime Minister.

BHUTTO. Well, Bob Cherry! I thought they wouldn't fill the streets for me again!

CHERRY *(grins and groans)*. Forget that. It's the Lahore summer that's driving me crazy. Where do you get the energy?

Cherry flops onto a floor cushion, wiping the sweat from his face with a big hanky. Khalid carries over a glass of water. Cherry downs it in a second.

CHERRY. Why the hell don't they organize coups in the winter?

General laughter.

CHERRY *(cont'd)*. I've just sent a despatch back home. 'Deposed leader still popular.'

BHUTTO. Will they publish it?

CHERRY. Our press still has some freedom. Remember Watergate!

Scene 53

EXTERIOR. MODEST BUNGALOW IN LAHORE.

There is still a small crowd of Bhutto supporters outside the house in excited mood. An unmarked car draws up. There are two uniformed officers inside: The Colonel and a Major. They step out uneasily, having observed the crowd.

BYSTANDER (*moving aggressively to officers*). Madr chod, ghaddar. You get out.

Colonel and Major touch their holsters.

CROWD (*chants*). Bhutto zindabad!

The Major is hit on the head with a stone.

COLONEL (*angry*). Move back you bastards. Bloody savages. Goondas.

He pushes them aside and he and Major walk towards the bungalow.

Scene 54

INTERIOR. LIVING ROOM, BUNGALOW IN LAHORE. DAY.

The conversation is interrupted by a loud knock on the door. Everyone is silent. Old friend walks to the door, sound of voices. He returns followed by two Army officers. They see Bhutto and, semi-automatically, are about to salute but they recover quickly. Bhutto smiles.

BHUTTO. Colonel. What is it now?

Colonel stares at the rest.

BHUTTO (*cont'd*). Ah, you want us to be alone?

Others leave voluntarily.

BHUTTO (*cont'd*). You see, your thought is their command.

COLONEL. The Chief Martial Law Administrator has sent me. You've broken your pledge. The crowd in Lahore was a provocation.

BHUTTO (*angry*). I don't care what you think. It's your job to make sure the people are whipped into submission. Don't blame me for your failure.

COLONEL. The General wants a meeting with you.

BHUTTO. When?

COLONEL. Tomorrow. We suggest you arrive by the late-night flight and treat this as a matter of highest security.

BHUTTO (*cold*). I'll see him tomorrow evening. Surely you rank a bit high to act as a simple messenger boy?

Colonel and aide stare angrily at Bhutto and leave. Others re-enter.

BHUTTO. Zia's livid about the reception today.

Cries of 'Oh oh' . . . and some laughter.

BHUTTO (*cont'd*). Wants me to take the midnight plane to Islamabad.

KHALID. Impossible, sir!

Bhutto calms him with a patient gesture.

BHUTTO. Doesn't make any difference. He's got 90 days. Then what?

CHERRY. I hate to think.

BHUTTO (*looks at him, pauses for reflection*). I know what you're thinking, Bob. He'll postpone elections. Possible. Danger for him is that we are building up a head of steam. People will be outraged.

CHERRY (*equally thoughtful*). For the steam to be properly utilized, you need an engine.

Bhutto is about to speak, but Cherry stops him.

CHERRY (*cont'd*). Hang on a minute. The people are the engine.

Bhutto nods vigorously with a smile.

CHERRY *(cont'd)*. And who is the piston?

Laughter as Bhutto silently points to his heart.

CHERRY *(cont'd)*. Agreed. Without the piston will the
engine function or not?

*Silence, as every face becomes serious, aware of the gravity of
the remark.*

Scene 55

EXTERIOR. ROAD. FLAGSTAFF HOUSE. JUST AFTER SUNSET.

Bhutto is in a private car being driven to Flagstaff House. Car approaches Zia's residence, halts outside gate. Soldier on duty walks to driver and peers in, then runs back and lifts a phone. Bhutto, kept waiting, smiles to himself. Soldier returns and signals to them to drive in. Car drives to porch. Two gardeners on the lawn stare at Bhutto. From the terrace, Mrs Zia, her head covered in dupatta, peeps at the former Prime Minister. Car arrives at porch. Driver jumps out and opens the door for Bhutto. Zia's ADC is waiting, nods curtly and indicates that Bhutto should follow him. Bhutto goes into the house.

Scene 56

FLAGSTAFF HOUSE. AUSTERE LIVING ROOM. NIGHT

There is a photograph of Zia with King Hussein of Jordan, with a group of fellow officers and one with Bhutto. Bhutto enters the room, looks first to see if the picture is still there and is slightly surprised to see that it is. He shakes hands with Zia who has stood up to receive him. Both men sit down. The atmosphere is extremely tense.

ZIA. Welcome to this house again. I am sad it is in new circumstances.

BHUTTO (*smiling*). Politics is always volatile in this country. Was there any particular reason for this invitation?

ZIA (*self-consciously lights a cigarette*). Just a talk. There are some problems.

BHUTTO (*raising eyebrows*). Oh?

ZIA. Your speeches, especially the one in Lahore, well . . . it's not what we expected.

BHUTTO. Why? Don't you expect me to participate in the elections? After all we've only got 90 days!

ZIA. Yes, yes, I know. But some of us feel that in Lahore you went too far.

BHUTTO (*angry but cool*). You and your Generals must

make up your minds. When you released me I asked: 'Am I allowed to campaign?'

ZIA. Oh yes, of course. Like everyone else.

BHUTTO. Ah! That's the problem. How can I, when millions come to hear me? The others give tea parties, hold press conferences. I speak to the people. They are the ones with the vote.

ZIA. I have always respected you.

Bhutto smiles wearily.

ZIA (*cont'd*). You don't believe me, but it's true. I assure you.

BHUTTO (*a sudden burst of anger*). Don't give me all this respect business. You have a nice way of showing it. Surrounding my house with tanks at midnight. Respect! I call it treason! Let's be open.

Zia stares at him.

BHUTTO (*cont'd*). I want to win the election. You know now that I will. You are in power. So there will be no rigging. But I will win.

ZIA (*grins*). You haven't changed at all. Look Bhutto-sahib. I have problems. Some of the Generals are worried. A gesture of goodwill will be appreciated. Why don't you go to your estates in Larkana and rest for a while?

Bhutto frowns. Zia pauses.

ZIA (*cont'd*). Why big meetings everywhere? Just relax
till the elections.

BHUTTO. I'm beginning to understand. You're worried
that people might become too active. Take matters
into their own hands. Get out of control. Surely,
the public hangings and floggings you have introduced will keep them quiet? Will they not,
General? Your new Islamic punishments should do
the trick?

ZIA (*stern*). Don't react like that. I say things for your
own good.

BHUTTO. Like the tanks? They were for my own good?
Like the brutalities in your prisons? They are for
the people's good? When are you going to release
Rashid and other members of my Party? This
bloody election is really like an obstacle race as far
as I am concerned. You want more obstacles?
(*Sticks out his tongue*) Why not remove this tongue?
I'm sure your mullahs will find something from the
Holy Book to justify the act. Eh? What do you want
from me? If you're worried, why did you release
me in the first place?

ZIA (*angry, the old mask has dropped forever*). You talk as if
you're still in power! Understand one thing, Mr

Bhutto! Army is in control. We will make Pakistan and Islamic state a reality.

Bhutto nods cynically.

ZIA. I said to you kindly, 'Go to Larkana.' You refused. Perhaps you should go abroad for a long rest. You have many friends in Europe. Take a long leave.

BHUTTO (*looks at him—then*). We'll talk again after 90 days, General Zia. Rest assured, I'm returning to my house in Karachi today. Nowhere else. I will fight the election like every other politician. You can't deny me that.

Bhutto stands up. Walks to the door without shaking hands. Turns round and looks at Zia who half rises but then sits back again and nods farewell.

BHUTTO. After 90 days, OK? We'll talk again. (*A look at Zia then he goes out.*)

ZIA (*softly, half to himself*). I don't think so.

Scene 57

INTERIOR. MILITARY GHQ. DAY.

Corps. Commanders' meeting. All present except Azad. Ifty and Rahman are more agitated than usual.

ZAMAN. He talked, like the old days. (*Grins*) He didn't listen.

ZAMAN. Like the old days!

ZIA. He will not compromise. He will not retire hurt. He will not accept your decision of leg before wicket. So we have to bowl him out. Clean bowled.

All laugh.

ZAMAN. Good idea, sir. But he has a good bat. He will not be bowled out.

ZIA. So?

ZAMAN. The ball has to be hurled at his head. One bumper after another.

NIZAMI. And don't forget, we appoint the umpires as well.

More laughter, then silence.

ZAMAN. We have to debar him from all political activity. There's no shortage of crimes. Corruption. Not a big problem. We could try him before a Special

Military Tribunal. Get some of his victims on tele-
vision. Send him before our officers. Verdict.
Guilty. Sentence—(*gestures with his hand across the
throat*).

IFTY. Are you crazy? We can't execute him for corruption.

ZAMAN. But our charge-sheet will grow and grow. *He*
blames Army for disaster of 1971 and Bangladesh
mess. *We* charge him with that supreme crime. He
was responsible for disintegration of Pakistan.
Charge is treason. We can do it. Our Intelligence
has much material.

NIZAMI. Timing is crucial.

ZAMAN. Agreed.

ZIA. Of course. Timing is always crucial in war. Wrong
move at wrong time and you can lose. To win a
match, the pitch has to be prepared well. We will
do what Zaman says, but slowly, till we're sure people will not respond. Slowly, slowly, but surely.
Zaman is right on solution. Method. Hmm. Must
think some more.

NIZAMI. Not for too long, sir. If Bhutto's meetings continue, we could have a civil war on our hands. He's
not yet gone to countryside. Landlords have started evicting peasants again. My gardener's brother
came weeping yesterday. Said he was thrown off

land. His owner said, 'Go to hell with Bhutto.' I
solved that problem quick, but . . .

ZAMAN. This is not common.

Scene 58

EXTERIOR. AIRPORT AT KARACHI. DAY

Bhutto's brand new Toyota. Driver holds opens the back door. Bhutto and Benazir get in. He lowers his window. A big crowd of supporters surround the car. Bhutto waves. Benazir gives a nervous, self-conscious wave. Many smile at her. The car drives off.

Scene 59

INTERIOR. BHUTTO'S CAR. DAY.

BENAZIR. What did he say?

Bhutto doesn't reply.

BENAZIR (*cont'd*). The house has been full of people.
Peasants, workers, students. Mummy says it's like
the old days

BHUTTO (*tired*). It's not the old days, Benazir. Mustn't
make that mistake. We have a new-style military
regime. They are ruthless. Bastards.

BENAZIR. What did he say, papa?

*Bhutto does not reply. Simply takes her hand and presses it
warmly.*

Scene 60

EXTERIOR. ZIA'S LAWN. FLAGSTAFF HOUSE. EARLY EVENING.

10th August 1977.

A table at the side with jugs of water, bottles of Pakola, 7-Up and a variety of other soft drinks. Zia and Mrs Zia are waiting for guests.

MRS ZIA. Finish him off. Now. Don't wait. If you wait too long you'll be finished. You know what they're saying in the bazaars. (*Pauses*) Two men. One coffin.

ZIA. Don't talk like this in front of our guests, please. Mushtaq is a judge.

The doorbell rings. Voices in the background. Mushtaq walks in. Mushtaq and Zia embrace. Mrs Zia salaams and exits. Soft drinks are served.

MUSHTAQ (*admiringly, but slightly tongue-in-cheek*). Chief Martial Law Administrator! Wonderful!

Smiles all round.

Scene 61

EXTERIOR. IMPOSING MANSION. EVENING.

A car approaches the mansion. The watchman sees the car and rushes to open the gate. He salaams enthusiastically as the car drives through. The gate is closed again.

Scene 62

INTERIOR. BHUTTO FAMILY HOME. EVENING.

A large and expensive mansion. Hussein is waiting in the hallway to receive Bhutto. Bhutto and Benazir walk in.

HUSSEIN. Welcome back. Bath? Massage?

Bhutto nods as Benazir disappears down a corridor.

HUSSEIN (*cont'd*). OK?

Bhutto nods, but Hussein knows him too well to believe it.

Scene 63

INTERIOR. LIVING ROOM. FLAGSTAFF HOUSE. EVENING.

Zia and Mushtaq are alone.

MUSHTAQ. We could re-open the case. Try him in a court of law. Charge: Murder.

ZIA. It's risky.

MUSHTAQ. I tell you it will stick. I know the law.

ZIA. Your plan is interesting, but Zaman must check it, OK?

MUSHTAQ. Check whatever you like. Murderers must not go unpunished. Must they?

ZIA. Of course not.

Scene 64

INTERIOR. DINING ROOM. BHUTTO'S HOUSE. NIGHT.

Everything is expensive. A long rectangular table of polished teak with comfortable chairs. The sideboard has expensive cut-glass displays. The table is set for three with wine glasses by every place. The floor is thickly carpeted. It is a more taste-ful and luxuriant affair than the PM's house in Islamabad. Bhutto, Nusrat and Benazir are eating. Hussein and two other servants are hovering in the background. Hussein exits through the pantry door. Other servants remain, standing motionless by the sideboard. Conversation takes place as if they didn't exist. Occasionally, they pour wine or water. When they observe an empty plate, they serve more food.

NUSRAT. I am worried. It's one thing suggesting you retire to Larkana. But a long holiday abroad. (*Her face clouds.*)

BHUTTO. He didn't like my reference to the 90 days.

BENAZIR. In what sense?

BHUTTO. I don't think they will permit an election. No. It makes sense now. A coup within a coup.

NUSRAT. What could they do?

BHUTTO. I've underestimated the bastard. Cherry was right. He was right.

Scene 65

EXTERIOR. KARACHI. NIGHT.

The night-watchman outside Bhutto's gate is sitting on a chair, nodding off. Suddenly, he is grabbed by two commandos in plain clothes. They overpower him and tie him up.

Scene 66

INTERIOR. BHUTTO'S BEDROOM. NIGHT.

Bhutto and Nusrat in bed, asleep.

Scene 67

EXTERIOR. KARACHI. NIGHT

3rd September 1977

An Army truck, led by a jeep, pulls up outside Bhutto's house. Colonel and a police officer get out of the jeep. Commandos in plain clothes pour out of the truck, armed with sten-guns and rifles.

Scene 68

INTERIOR. BHUTTO'S BEDROOM. NIGHT.

Darkness. Colonel shakes Bhutto. All the lights are suddenly switched on. He and Nusrat sit up in bed, bewildered, and see the invaders—12 commandos in the room. Nusrat pulls the covers to her neck. The bed is surrounded. Bhutto is about to shout.

COLONEL. Sir, we've come to arrest.

BHUTTO. Where's your warrant?

COLONEL. No, warrant. The country is under Martial Law.

BHUTTO. Will you leave the room while my wife gets dressed?

Scene 69

INTERIOR. BENAZIR'S BEDROOOM. NIGHT.

Lights are switched on. She opens her eyes and sees several armed intruders.

BENAZIR (*scared*). Who are you? Who are you?

Scene 70

INTERIOR. LANDING OUTSIDE BEDROOM. NIGHT.

Several armed men are waiting. Benazir walks out of her room followed by men. She stops on the landing.

BENAZIR (*to men on landing*). Look at what you are doing. Is this why my father had 90,000 soldiers released from India?

SOLDIER (*puzzled*). Miss. Whose house is this?

BENAZIR. You don't know? This is Bhutto's house. *Your* Prime Minister.

Soldiers look bewildered. Just then Bhutto, now dressed, is frog-marched out of his room onto the landing. Soldiers move to stand in front of Benazir.

BENAZIR (*cont'd*). Papa! Papa! Where are they taking you?

BHUTTO (*as he is taken downstairs*). Don't worry. Tell your brothers to stay abroad.

He is pushed forward by his captors. Suddenly the house is empty. Hussein staggers up the stairs, his face bruised and bloody.

BENAZIR. Did they beat you, old man?

Hussein nods.

HUSSEIN. You should see the cook's son. I'll send him
off to hospital.

*Suddenly, Nusrat walks out onto the landing. Pale and
shattered. Mother and daughter move towards each other and
embrace. Benazir weeps loudly. Nusrat silently.*

Scene 71

INTERIOR. PRISON ROOM IN LAHORE. DAY.

The room is dark except for a blue bulb. It contains a bed on which Bhutto is seated. Colonel enters. Bhutto recognizes him and a sneer appears on his face. The sound of soldiers goose-stepping outside can be heard.

COLONEL (*putting a piece of paper in front of Bhutto*). Will you sign this please?

BHUTTO (*scornful*). I never sign blank cheques.

COLONEL. If you do not cooperate the consequences will be painful.

BHUTTO (*angry*). Get out of the room. I don't have to suffer you. Intolerable wretch! Don't you dare threaten me with consequences. Get out! I have nothing to say. I want my lawyers.

Colonel goes to the door.

BHUTTO. Where are we? I mean which town?

COLONEL. Lahore.

BHUTTO. I thought so. What are you holding me for? What's the charge? What have they cooked up?

Colonel shakes his head implying he cannot speak and leaves the room.

Scene 72

EXTERIOR. PRISON COURTYARD. LAHORE. DAY.

Bakhtiar, Bhutto's lawyer, sits at the table with his papers.

BAKHTIAR. They are charging you under Section 120-B
of the Pakistan Penal Code for three offences.
Firstly, that you conspired with others in 1974 to
murder Ahmed Raza, then a member of the
National Assembly. Secondly, that you aided and
abetted in the murder of Raza's father, Ahmed
Khan, who was in the car carrying Raza on 10th
November 1974. Thirdly, that you aided and abetted
in the attempted murder of Ahmed Raza. Under
Section 302, you are charged with murder.

BHUTTO (*amazed*). Grotesque! A farce. No sane court
will accept this absurdity.

BAKHTIAR (*gently*). The punishment under Section 302
is death, sir.

BHUTTO. I know. They want to frighten me. Get me on
my knees to plead for mercy. They can go to hell!

Scene 73

EXTERIOR. LAWN. FLAGSTAFF HOUSE. TWILIGHT.

Table and chairs. Notebook and tape recorder on the table. As Cherry and Zia shake hands, a camera flashes.

CHERRY (*staring at departing cameraman*). What was that all about?

ZIA. You are a distinguished foreign correspondent. Our papers want a photograph of you interviewing me. (*Smiles*)

CHERRY (*formal throughout interview*). I see. Can we start?

Zia nods.

CHERRY (*cont'd*). Do you mind if I use my tape recorder?

ZIA. Go ahead.

Cherry switches it on.

CHERRY. General Zia. You swore your loyalty to the Constitution. Yet you overthrow an elected leader. You promised elections within 90 days. Five days ago you asked for another six months. What exactly are your plans?

ZIA. So many googlies and I haven't even got my bat in place. (*Grins*) I am a simple soldier, not a politician. We need more time to prepare the electoral register, check everything, make sure all the parties have the same rights. Then elections.

CHERRY. Do you seriously believe that Bhutto is a murderer? If so, why did you serve under him?

ZIA. I do not know if he's guilty. The Court will decide, Mr Cherry. But I was taken in by Bhutto. He charmed me like so many others, including you, I think? When I took over I saw all his files. I was disturbed and slightly disgusted. He kept secret files on all his own Cabinet Ministers. He interfered in everything. I was very shocked by my discoveries. How such a great man could behave in so low fashion on many trivial matters. On one such file, he wrote 'Zia is a simpleton.' I was his Chief of Staff and he wrote that? What did he do to others not so powerful? He could be responsible for murder. For anything.

Cherry switches off the tape recorder, puts down his notebook. Sips tea.

CHERRY. Could I ask you something off the record?

ZIA. Of course!

CHERRY. Is it necessary to treat him like this? Very few people take this murder charge seriously. The Chief Justice is known to loathe his guts. From your own point of view, surely, it's counter-productive?

ZIA. Listen. I offered him retirement from politics. I offered him permission to go abroad for a long stay. Exile. Whatever you call it. Did he respond? No! Arrogant man. Treated me as if I was a fool.

CHERRY. His application for bail comes up today. Are you going to stop it?

ZIA. No, no. I've told you, the courts decide. (*Grins*) *If* they give him bail that's up to them. It would be foolish but it would be up to them.

Cherry and Zia look at each other. Cherry tries to gauge what lies underneath. As Zia grins and half rises, Colonel rushes forward. Zia stops in his tracks.

COLONEL (*in a loud, breathless whisper*). Bhutto's been guaranteed bail, sir, by a High Court Bench!

Zia is shocked, but recovers quickly. Turns and smiles at Cherry.

ZIA. There, you see, Mr Cherry. Our judiciary is truly impartial.

Zia turns to go to the house.

Scene 74

EXTERIOR. BHUTTO'S RESIDENCE, KARACHI. DAY.

14th September 1977. Benazir, Nusrat and Bhutto are sitting on an outdoor sofa. Benazir is sitting on the grass with her head leaning against the sofa. Her father strokes her hair.

NUSRAT. But are you sure? Are you sure they won't go on?

BHUTTO (*sipping whisky*). Who can be sure? The Bench which approved the bail admitted all the flaws of the case. Samdani more or less said it was a farce.

BENAZIR. But Samdani isn't Chief Justice.

BHUTTO. Exactly.

At a distance we see Cherry, preceded by Hussein, walking towards the trio. He approaches the family, who all look happy to see him. Hussein pours him a whisky from an adjoining table.

BHUTTO. My dear Bob. Good to see you.

CHERRY. The news is not good.

Cherry sips his whisky.

BHUTTO. Come on. Come on. Out with it.

CHERRY. They will destroy you. Elections? Not for a long, long time. He's clever, this one. He's hoping to play politicians off against each other. Keep everyone guessing. Make uncertainties part of everyday life. They will put you away for life. I've been talking to them. The men in the Embassy. 'Bhutto's finished,' they say. 'Forget him.'

BHUTTO. Let them try, Bob. Let them try. You don't have to tell me what these bastards are doing to my country. Zia's got to do it to someone, I suppose, with a wife like that.

NUSRAT. Zulfikar! Shocking! (*She smiles, nevertheless.*)

CHERRY. I'm glad you haven't lost your sense of humour.

Hussein walks in and whispers in Bhutto's ear. This annoys Nusrat.

NUSRAT. Stop whispering, Hussein. Mr Cherry is a friend. Speak.

BHUTTO. Azad is outside! Alone. (*To Hussein*) Bring him in.

Cherry rises. Bhutto signals him to sit. As Azad approaches the group, Bhutto rises slowly and stares at him. Azad salutes, even though he is in civvies.

BHUTTO. Are you on official business?

AZAD. No. As a friend.

BHUTTO. Where was your friendship when the bastard was plotting to overthrow me?

AZAD. I know. I should have come to you but somehow
they prevented it. I was trapped. Trapped. Then
Whiskey told us you were planning to behead us all.

BHUTTO. So it was him. It was a lie. Why are you here?
You could get into trouble.

AZAD. No, no. I've just resigned my post. They were
buggering me around. 'Go to Saudi Arabia.' 'Go to
Abu Dhabi.' 'Go here.' 'Go there.' Best to get out.
Now I'll break the law by drinking a whisky.

*All laugh. Hussein brings the bottle and the whisky is poured
and consumed. Then they see how troubled Azad looks.*

BHUTTO. Well?

AZAD. Leave the country. Tonight. Tomorrow.

*Bhutto, Nusrat and Benazir exchange looks with Cherry. A
General's warning is far more official.*

BHUTTO. Why?

AZAD. Zaman wants you polished off. He wanted it
before the coup. I stopped it then. Now there are
no barriers. Trial's a complete farce. Everything is
planned.

BHUTTO. How can everything be planned? The people
have the capacity to upset many plans.

AZAD. I agree, so do Zia and Zaman. But they noticed
something. When Martial Law was declared noth-

ing happened. Not a bird twittered. They laughed about it.

BHUTTO. Not a bird twittered? What about the textile workers in Multan? They went on strike. Zia's machine guns ended that. Sixty workers killed. Hundreds wounded.

AZAD. That's small beer, my friend. The Army was preparing to deal with a General Strike. It never happened. Don't resist now. Save yourself.

BHUTTO. More important to save Pakistan.

CHERRY. Are the two not connected?

BHUTTO. Of course they are. That's why I won't run. Let them do their worst. Finally they will run.

Scene 75

INTERIOR. MILITARY GHQ. NIGHT.

Corps. Commanders' meeting. Azad is absent. The mood is tense.

ZIA (*angry*). I want him back behind bars.

ZAMAN. With respect, sir, I told you that if we let civilian courts take over there could be a problem.

Zia glowers.

ZAMAN (*cont'd*). This Samdani fellow is the bloody problem. Mushtaq won't pick him for a judge for the trial but he's damaged the case by his remarks. He will not revoke the bail.

ZIA. I want Bhutto back in prison tomorrow. We can't let this bird fly away now.

NIZAM. Then, we'll re-arrest him.

IFTIKHAR. How?

NIZAMI. Special Martial Law Regulation No. 12. Authorities have unlimited power to arrest anyone for three months to prevent them acting in a manner prejudicial to the purpose for which Martial Law was proclaimed or to the security of Pakistan.

ZIA. Arrest him again tonight. I want the trial to begin.

Scene 76

INTERIOR. KOT LAKHPAT JAIL, OUTSIDE LAHORE. DAY.

An old prison built during the Raj. Bhutto is in a Class 1 cell, a largish room with windows, relatively clean, furnished with a bed, table and chair. Outside the window we see prisoners walking and dozens of police guards. Bhutto is sitting on the bed with Nusrat and Benazir. His chief lawyer, Bakhtiar, is seated at the table. While they are talking, we can hear the sound of a prisoner being whipped. Every time the whip hits the man (10 in all), the three stop talking.

BHUTTO (*in charge*). Don't worry about this murder case. It's a complete fraud. A farce. A distraction designed to cover up their own crimes.

Whipping sound. A man's groans are heard.

BHUTTO (*cont'd*). This is unbearable. Barbaric.

BENAZIR. They're doing it in public, every week. Hangings and floggings. Yesterday, in front of a big crowd, a man who was being whipped refused to scream. With every whiplash, he shouted 'Long Live Bhutto.' The Army Officer supervising the operation went mad. 'Hit him harder,' he shouted. The flogger did, but the man was unbowed. His back was bleeding. Raw. Skin falling off. He kept

123

shouting. They had to stop finally. The crowd had been silent. In the end it began to applaud. A few slogans too. The police broke up the crowd.

BHUTTO. It's going to get worse. Much worse. Nusrat. (*He pauses, they look at each other*) You don't have to remain in public. Others can take over. It might be better if you went to Larkana.

NUSRAT (*stroking his face*). You know I can't. The Acting Chairman of the Party?

Bhutto smiles.

NUSRAT (*cont'd*). You have become a symbol. Bhutto. Bhutto. The name is on everyone's lips. The Party was you. Nothing else. You made it. They need your name, that's why I agreed. Let them do their worst. All the children want to fight back. The boys ring every day. Want your permission to come back.

BHUTTO (*firm*). No!

NUSRAT. That's what I said. Anyway, don't you dare exile me to Larkana. Anything's better than that.

Both laugh.

BHUTTO (*to Benazir*). Maybe you should leave for a while, darling. Go back to Oxford or anywhere. Study. Get a doctorate. Get away from here.

BENAZIR. No! No! No! The women are going to fight back. We will not go into hiding. We must be seen by the people. A peasant woman came to see me yesterday. The Mullah had told her 'Bhutto's mother wasn't a Muslim.'

BHUTTO. Bastard!

NUSRAT. You know what the woman asked in return? 'And was the Prophet Mohammed's mother a Muslim?'

All laugh and tears well up in Bhutto's eyes.

Scene 77

INTERIOR. COURTROOM. MORNING.

6th October 1977. High Court in session.

Five judges constitute the Bench. Mushtaq will sit in the centre. The court functions as in Britain.

A special dock, more a roofless cage, has been erected for Bhutto. The courtroom is packed. Nusrat and Benazir are sitting just behind Bhutto's lawyers. Cherry and Lily are on the Press bench

As Bhutto walks in with guards, over half the court rises in respect. He waves and is taken to the cage. His lawyers walk over to exchange a few words. He is dressed in a smart suit and looks well.

CLERK OF THE COURT. The Court will rise.

All rise. Judges enter. Mushtaq glares at Bhutto. All sit.

CLERK OF THE COURT. The prisoner will stand.

Bhutto stands up.

CLERK OF THE COURT. Zulfikar Ali Bhutto, you are charged that at some time in 1974, you conspired with Abdul Mahmud, an Approver in this case, and others to countenance the murder of Ahmed Raza, then a member of the National Assembly, through the agency of the Federal Security Force. You are further charged that you aided and abetted the other accused in this case to carry out this conspiracy. You are further charged of aiding and abetting in the murder of Raza's father Ahmed Khan, on 10th November 1974. How do you plead?

BHUTTO. Not guilty.

MUSHTAQ. You may sit down.

Bhutto sits.

MUSHTAQ (*cont'd*). The Prosecution will proceed.

We see only Bhutto.

PUBLIC PROSECUTOR. M'lud, this is a sad day for our country. A former Prime Minister is on trial for murder. A common criminal. As I unfold this sordid and murky case many of you will find the facts difficult to believe but our witnesses are all present. They tell a sad story. This man you see before you . . .

Dissolve.

Scene 78

INTERIOR. COURTROOM. DAY.

Mahmud, an Approved, once Bhutto's Chief of Police, is in the witness box.

BAKHTIAR. I repeat what I asked you three times yesterday. What made you turn Approver? Were you subjected to military pressure when in prison? Have you been promised anything?

PROSECUTION. M'lud, this is irrelevant.

MUSHTAQ. Sustained.

BHUTTO (*standing up*). This is a kangaroo court.

MUSHTAQ. Sit down, you!

BHUTTO. Your bias is obvious.

MUSHTAQ. I'll have you removed if you make a nuisance. (*To Defence Counsel*) Why are you staring at me?

Murmur in court.

MUSHTAQ (*cont'd*). This remark cannot be reported in the Press.

Dissolve.

Scene 79

INTERIOR. COURTROOM. DAY.

Judges in court.

In camera.

MUSHTAQ. You may begin

BHUTTO. I appeal to the Court to transfer this trial to
another Bench. Your behaviour has been a disgrace. I cannot and do not expect a fair trial from
this Court. You have hampered the Defence in
Court, the Chief Justice has given press conferences on the case to foreign journalists, there have
been secret meetings between Chief Justice and
Chief Martial Law Administrator. Yes, I know you
are old friends. This is not a murder trial. It is a
political vendetta.

MUSHTAQ. We've heard enough. (*Consults other judges
rapidly.*) Petition to move case dismissed.

Scene 80

INTERIOR. PRISON CELL.

Nusrat and Bhutto are alone. He is stroking her hand.
Suddenly, he kisses it.

BHUTTO. I can't bear the thought of you and Benazir
suffering.

NUSRAT (*smiling*). It's nothing compared to what they're
doing to you.

BHUTTO. It's not me they're destroying. It's an idea.
They want to show the poor—'Look, this man used
to talk about you. Tell you fairytales about ending
oppression. Look where he is now. If we can treat
him like this, who are you? You are nothing. Ants
to be ground into the dust.'

NUSRAT. Mushtaq's behaviour has been attacked in the
Western press.

BHUTTO. Mushtaq! He's an instrument. It's the Army
which took the decision. I hear you're beginning to
make powerful speeches.

NUSRAT (*laughs*). Don't tease. They insisted I become
Acting Chairman of the Party.

BHUTTO. They were right. You've more guts than all

the rest of them. What news of Khalid and Akbar? Still locked up?

Nusrat nods.

BHUTTO (*cont'd*). One thing we must never do. Never!

Nusrat looks at him.

BHUTTO (*cont'd*). Go down on our knees and plead for mercy. Never.

Suddenly the cell door is flung open and a posse of policemen arrives. They walk up to the couple.

NUSRAT. Oh my God. What now?

POLICE OFFICER (*handing her a paper*). Mrs Bhutto. Here is a warrant for your arrest. Please come with us.

Bhutto and Nusrat embrace.

BHUTTO. Where is my wife being taken?

POLICE OFFICER. It's only house arrest, sir. Come along please.

Nusrat leaves.

Scene 81

INTERIOR. COURTROOM. LAHORE. DAY.

Bhutto is led to the dock. It is 8.30 a.m. An empty Court.
Judges enter in a hurry. Second judge will read the judgement.

MUSHTAQ. Zulfikar Ali Bhutto, son of Shanawaza
Bhutto of Larkana, Sind. We have reached a judgement. It is unanimous. We have found you guilty
on all charges of which you stand accused. We find
that you are a compulsive liar. You have wrecked
the country, damaged its standing. You are a
Muslim only in name. In fact you are such a person who in all probability would destroy the very
basis of the Constitution and the law which you are
sworn to uphold. All the offences with which you
were charged are proved to the hilt. Your com-
plaints against the Court are demented products
of falsehood and your imagination . . . This Court
sentences you to seven years imprisonment on the
first charge for attempt to murder, five years
imprisonment on the second charge for
conspiracy to kill and death for the conspiracy to
murder which resulted in the death of the victim's
father. You will hang by the neck until you are
dead.

Scene 82

EXTERIOR. GRAND TRUNK ROAD. DAY.

A car, its roof rack laden with suitcases, is seen travelling fast. Inside, Nusrat and Benazir are sitting, pale-faced and tired. They have not slept.

Scene 83

INTERIOR. CAR. DAY.

BENAZIR (*clutching her mother's hand*). They can't mean
it, mummy. Can they? They're just putting him in
the death cell to frighten us.

Scene 84

EXTERIOR. RAWALPINDI JAIL.

We establish exterior of prison. Place and year flash:

Rawalpindi Jail, 1978.

Scene 85

INTERIOR. DEATH CELL, RAWALPINDI. DAY.

Bhutto wakes up. He is sweating profusely. He has lost over two stone and appears tired and gaunt. There are sores on his lips. The death cell has no window. Bhutto wipes sweat off his face on his shirt sleeve. Then he gets up, pours himself a glass of water from an earthenware vessel at the foot of the bed. Then lies down on the bed. His eyes are wide open. He hears the cell door being unlocked, but does not turn around to look.

Nusrat and Benazir enter. The door is relocked. She walks to the bed and stands, looking down at him. He turns around, sees her.

NUSRAT (*softly*). I thought you were asleep.

BHUTTO. I had an awful dream. Couldn't sleep at all.

She sits on the bed and strokes his hair.

BHUTTO (*cont'd*). You. How are you?

She smiles.

BHUTTO (*cont'd*). The children?

NUSRAT. Fine. Send their love . . . Zulfy, time is pressing. We have to decide today on the appeal.

BHUTTO. Pointless bloody exercise. What's the use?

NUSRAT. We gain time. That's important. Isn't it?

Bhutto shrugs his shoulders.

NUSRAT (*cont'd*). What's wrong with you? We must fight. Supreme Court may be useless, but it's our only Court of Appeal.

BHUTTO. Our only Court of Appeal in history.

BENAZIR. Please. This is no time for heroics, papa. Everyone wants you to appeal. Please let us instruct our lawyers today.

BHUTTO. You want to witness another farce? Look how the bastard Mushtaq, arselicker, treated me in Lahore. Zia's poodle! The New Chief Justice of the Supreme Court is the same. Spare me the humiliation.

NUSRAT. You've had your own way. Always. With every-one. Your children and your wife are now pleading with you, Zulfy. I've kept quiet till now. Please think of us. I won't let you go. I won't. I'm instruct-ing our lawyers to file the appeal. (*Takes out the let-ter from her bag*) I want you to sign this now. Please. Please.

Bhutto softens and strokes her face. Without a word he takes the pen from her and signs. She hugs him and weeps.

Scene 86

INTERIOR. MILITARY GHQ. NIGHT.

ZAMAN. Let's assume the worst. They acquit him. He walks out a free man.

ZIA. It won't happen.

ZAMAN. But if it did. They could uphold the Appeal on some technical ground.

ZIA. Then we can try him for a hundred other crimes. This time a military court.

Nizami smiles, but Zaman frowns.

ZAMAN. We might have to do that sir, but it would look very bad.

Scene 87

INTERIOR. SUPREME COURT IN SESSION. DAY.

20th May 1978. There are seven judges on the bench, three on either side of the Chief Justice. The Court is packed. Cherry and Lily are among the Press. The atmosphere is dignified and courteous, quite unlike the High Court.

BAKHTIAR. M'luds, the case of the Prosecution in the High Court was, as I shall show, full of inconsistencies, contradictions and circumstantial evidence. With your permission, I will briefly state the main point on which our Appeal to this Court is based.

Judges nod.

BAKHTIAR (*cont'd*). There are three main grounds.

Chief Justice taking copious notes, nods politely to Bakhtiar.

BAKHTIAR (*cont'd*). It is a false, fabricated and politically motivated case . . . a case of international conspiracy of which Mr Zulfikar Ali Bhutto is the victim. He was forcibly ejected from office. The aim of the military junta is his political and physical elimination.

CHIEF JUSTICE. Political and physical?

BAKHTIAR. Yes, My Lord.

JUDGE 2. Political elimination?

BAKHTIAR. Yes, M'lud, and physical. My second ground
of attack is that he was tried by a thoroughly hostile and biased Bench.

JUDGE 3. Pardon?

BAKHTIAR. Biased and hostile Bench

JUDGE 3. Biased and . . .

BAKHTIAR. Hostile. He did not get a fair trial. For that
reason he has no option but to boycott the proceedings. For two months he tried to defend himself. The Bench of the High Court made this task
impossible. The behaviour and bias of the Chief
Justice of the High Court was a scandal and a
disgrace.

Judges take notes.

BAKHTIAR (*cont'd*). Thirdly, My Lords, leaving all else
aside, the actual evidence is based exclusively on
hearsay. Literally. The Appellant was condemned
because of orders supposedly given on the telephone! It is unacceptable evidence even if we
ignore that those testifying for the Prosecution
were all Approvers in the case.

CHIEF JUSTICE (*very courteous*). Please continue, Mr
Bakhtiar.

Scene 88

EXTERIOR. COURTYARD. SUPREME COURT. DAY.

Chief Justice is strolling in the winter sun with the Tall Judge.

CHIEF JUSTICE. We are the lawmakers, my friend. We must uphold the law.

TALL JUDGE. I agree, but the whole prosecution case was a fraud. Bakhtiar's right. Mushtaq's behaviour was despicable. He should be debarred from the Bench. You know that as well as me.

CHIEF JUSTICE. You are amazing. Bhutto denied you an extension. Stopped your promotion. You are generous.

TALL JUDGE (*angry*). But we are the lawmakers, My Lord. Personal or political prejudices must not stand in the way. He is innocent.

The two men stroll in silence for a few seconds. Then:

CHIEF JUSTICE. Of course he's innocent, but the national interest demands his head.

They stop walking and stare at each other.

CHIEF JUSTICE (*cont'd*). Without a state there is no law. Bhutto alive means chaos, confusion. Maybe even revolution.

TALL JUDGE. So this is what things have come to now! We are not judges, but butchers. Doing the Army's dirty work. I will resist, My Lord.

CHIEF JUSTICE. Do so, but it is useless . . . One more thing. Isn't your nephew in the Army?

TALL JUDGE. What of it?

CHIEF JUSTCE. At least think of his future . . .

Scene 89

INTERIOR. DEATH CELL. DAY.

Bhutto and Nusrat are alone in the cell. It is their last meeting, though neither is aware of it. Nusrat is under enormous strain which she attempts to conceal from him.

BHUTTO. It will be strange to go outside again. See old familiar faces, a friend here, an enemy there. Have they agreed to let Hussein bring my clothes?

NUSRAT (*smiling*). Yes, yes, Hussein will be here on time. He's like a lost dog. Desperate to see you. (*Pause*) The lawyers are confident. Two judges have been friendly.

BHUTTO (*cynical*). Two out of seven? Two have been 'retired.' One of them was a decent sort. Zia's reducing the odds all the time. I have no illusions Nusrat. None. I've been thinking. About you, the children . . . the country.

NUSRAT. Don't, Zulfy. No.

BHUTTO. Even if they kill me, keep the boys out. I don't want their lives ruined. No time for sentimentality.

A tear crawls down Nusrat's face.

BHUTTO (*cont'd*). My wife. Without you I would have been dead now. At least inside myself. I would have been lost. Sometimes I curse myself for involving you and Benazir.

NUSRAT. Shush. Stop it. We are doing what we are, because we have to. (*Strokes his face*) My Chairman.

Both smile. They see the warder standing waiting. Bhutto signals to him to wait.

BHUTTO. Whatever happens, Nusrat, none of us must demean ourselves. Understand?

She is silent.

BHUTTO (*cont'd*). Nusrat, this is important. No one from my family must plead for mercy before this usurper. Never. Promise me! You must!

She looks at him and nods.

Scene 90

EXTERIOR. GARDEN, FLAGSTAFF HOUSE. DAY.

Late at night. Zia and the Chief Justice are sitting close to each other on the sofa, sipping tea and talking in low voices.

ZIA. You must understand. I'm not concerned for myself. Let him abuse me. No problem. But if he starts divulging state secrets to discredit Army, stop him immediately and remove him from Court . . .

CHIEF JUSTICE. The foreign press will be there!

ZIA. To hell with them. Their masters know what's going on. (*Grins*)

CHIEF JUSTICE. Leave it to my discretion. Don't worry. Mushtaq mishandled the whole case in High Court. His diatribes were a disgrace.

ZIA. Another thing. You're sure you have a majority?

Chief Justice nods.

ZIA (*cont'd*). Hundred per cent sure?

Chief Justice nods again.

ZIA (*cont'd*). Good. Good.

CHIEF JUSTICE. There is only one problem . . .

Zia looks at him.

CHIEF JUSTICE (*cont'd*). Even my judges are worried. They think you won't hold elections. If they thought you wouldn't allow free elections, the reason you say you took over, we might not get a majority to dispose of Bhutto.

ZIA (*smiling*). I assure you I am not putting on a show. If I want political power, what is there stopping me? The Army is behind me. I could do what I like. What is the Constitution? I could tear it up. Say we shall live under a different system. Who could stop me? Most of the politicians would follow, their tails wagging. I don't do any of this. Judge-sahib, tell your fellow judges that Zia has no political ambitions. Personally, I am not interested in political office and shall never accept one. I give you my word.

CHIEF JUSTICE. There will be no problems.

He rises. So does Zia. Both men shake hands warmly and embrace.

Scene 91

INTERIOR. DEATH CELL. DAY.

Bhutto is getting dressed. He is putting on an expensive Saville Row suit while Hussein is polishing his shoes. The clothes are laid out on the ramshackle bed and contrast grotesquely with the surroundings. Nonetheless, Bhutto is in a chirpy mood. He pulls on his trousers.

HUSSEIN. Oh my God. My God!

BHUTTO. What's wrong?

HUSSEIN. Wrong? Can't you see? The trousers are too loose. What have they done to you? (*He sheds a tear.*)

BHUTTO. Did you bring me a cigar?

Hussein nods silently and hands one to him.

Bhutto puts on a jacket. The clothes hang loosely on him, showing how much weight he has lost. His cheeks, usually puffy, are now almost emaciated.

Hussein takes out a matchbox to light the cigar.

Bhutto is sitting on the bed. Hussein stands. Bhutto pulls him down so he is sitting as well, next to his master. Bhutto bites the cigar-end and spits it out. Hussein lights the cigar. Bhutto inhales in obvious delight. As he exhales, it is almost as if both men are hidden by smoke in the tiny cell.

Scene 92

EXTERIOR. SUPREME COURT. DAY.

A car arrives. A few of Bhutto's followers chant. Bhutto gets out of the car and is hustled inside by two policemen.

Scene 93

INTERIOR. SUPREME COURT. SAME DAY.

The Supreme Court is packed as never before. Cherry and Lily and other foreign journalists are present. As Bhutto enters, there is silence. Bhutto looks slightly dazed. He is taken and seated next to the Defence lawyers. Then the judges enter and everyone rises. The Chief Justice stares hard at Bhutto, who trembles slightly. All sit.

CHIEF JUSTICE. There is no reason to delay the matter further. Mr Bhutto, you may address the Court.

Bhutto, pale and shaken, rises and moves to podium. The tension is visible. Pindrop silence.

BHUTTO. My Lords, I thank you for permitting me to defend myself. A right which I have been denied for a long time. I am grateful to Your Lordships, for a lot more is at stake than my life. My reputation, my political career, the honour and future of my family and above all, yes, above all, the future of Pakistan itself is involved. This is my view. I am here because I believe in my innocence and because I hope that this Court will give me justice. The eyes of the world are on this trial. It is not

often that an elected Prime Minister is tried for
the crime of murder. My person is of little importance. Gentlemen, this will be the most important
trial of your lives as well. For history is the most
punishing judge of all. Its verdict cannot be
challenged. (*Wipes forehead, sips water.*)

Scene 94

TIME LAPSE. 19TH DECEMBER 1978. DAY.

BHUTTO. The High Court decision was a farce. That judgement was biased and insulting. I don't like being insulted. I remember when I was at Christchurch College, Oxford. My tutor advised me to take three rather than two years to study jurisprudence. 'Even an English boy,' he said 'would need that.' As an Asian, I felt slighted. I insisted on taking it in two years, and passed with honours. I was told by the High Court that I was a Muslim in name only, I was a compulsive liar, remarks were thrown in about my temperament. This was more like a vendetta by a fundamentalist sect than a balanced judgement. Religion for me is a matter between an individual and his God . . . My Lords, I have been a member of the National Assembly for over two decades, I am used to being attacked in Parliament. I am not so thin-skinned that I would have an opponent as slight as an accuser murdered.

Scene 95

TIME LAPSE. 20TH DECEMBER 1978. DAY.

BHUTTO. My Lords . . .

Bhutto now appears utterly exhausted. Sweat pours down his face.

BHUTTO (*cont'd*). I have been shabbily treated since my arrest 15 months ago. In Lahore they put 50 lunatics in the adjoining cells. They screamed all night. They turned off my water for 21 days. When I was first brought to prison here, they used to throw pebbles on the roof every 15 minutes. Collect them in the morning and throw them the next night. The military guards on the parapet next to the cell used to jump with their boots on the tin roof. I thought last night they would spare me. They did not. I am not a rootless phenomenon. For 90 days I have not seen sunshine or light. Only a sick and depraved regime could have treated me like this. Can I go on? I am in your hands.

CHIEF JUSTICE. You can speak as long as you like, but please be relevant.

BHUTTO. Thank you.

Scene 96

TIME LAPSE. 22ND DECEMBER 1978. DAY.

BHUTTO. My Lords. Your responsibility is an awesome one, for by your verdict you can end the nightmare that haunts our country. You can show our people that political bias is alien to our Judiciary. You can salvage the lost honour of this country and make the real perpetrators of this grotesque trial hang their heads in shame. I was advised to leave the country by my friends, including former Generals. I refused to run away, I wanted my people to know that I would fight till the end. That is why I am standing before you. Your Lordships have been kind in giving me this hearing. I did not expect it of you. Everyone who is made of flesh and bones has to leave this world one day. Now you can hang me.

Scene 97

INTERIOR. MILITARY GHQ. DAY.

Zia, Zaman and Nizami. Zia is seated on the table. Nizami and Zaman sitting. Zia stands up, paces up and down.

ZIA. The minute the verdict is announced, arrest every potential troublemaker. Whip them if necessary. If we survive the first week after the verdict, then I'm sure we'll ride the crisis.

NIZAMI. Intelligence reports indicate some discontent among the soldiers, sir.

ZIA (*brushes this aside with a gesture*). I don't believe it.

ZAMAN. When does the Court decide?

ZIA. They're meeting now.

Scene 98

INTERIOR. JUDGES' CHAMBERS. DAY.

All the seven judges are present. The atmosphere is tense.

TALL JUDGE. There is no case, My Lords.

SECOND JUDGE. The evidence against Bhutto is more than ample.

TALL JUDGE. What . . . are you crazy?

CHIEF JUSTICE. The statements of two Approvers are supported by a mass of oral and documentary evidence.

TALL JUDGE. None of it would convict the accused in any civilized country. It's all circumstantial. No real evidence. The Approvers were totally unreliable and contradictory.

Scene 99

INTERIOR. MILITARY GHQ.

All present as before.

ZIA. We should try and get him to sign a confession.

ZAMAN. We've tried. It's useless.

NIZAMI. Chief is right. One more try.

Zaman looks at Zia, who nods.

SHORT JUDGE. The trial and the High Court are a travesty of justice. (*To Tall Judge*) You are absolutely right. There is not a single piece of direct evidence to implicate Bhutto in the murder of Raza's father. Everything is circumstantial, hearsay. As Prime Minister, this man was the head of government. Does every misdemeanour, regardless of who carried it out, rest on him? That would make a mockery of justice, at least according to our norms of jurisprudence. Let's not bring the Supreme Court into disrepute.

CHIEF JUSTICE. Calm down, my friend. There is one precedent. The Nurembourg Tribunal. Justice Jackson refused to exonerate the leaders of Germany simply because the actual crimes had been committed by subordinates.

TALL JUDGE. This is not the case of the Prosecution, sir.
They allege a conspiracy to kill one person.
There's no talk of collective crimes of genocide.

CHIEF JUSTICE. It's pointless debating any more. The
lines are drawn. So it will be a split verdict. How
many people believe he's guilty?

Three judges raise hands. Pause. Then a fourth.

CHIEF JUSTICE (*cont'd*). So be it.

TALL JUDGE. A 4-3 split, My Lords. Not good if the
Army wants to hang him.

He stares hard at the Chief Justice.

Scene 100

INTERIOR. GHQ. DAY.

ADC gives Zia a letter. He opens it. Reads it. His expression gives nothing away. He hands the letter to Nizami. He reads it, looks at Zia, hands it to Zaman.

Scene 101

INTERIOR. NUSRAT BHUTTO'S DETENTION HOUSE. NIGHT.

3rd April 1978.

Nusrat and Benazir are sitting on a sofa. Hussein enters.

HUSSEIN. It's the police!

Mother and daughter look at each other and instinctively hold hands. Chief of Police enters room.

POLICE CHIEF. Please get ready.

NUSRAT. Both of us?

POLICE CHIEF. Yes.

BENAZIR. It's the last time? (*Her voice breaks*).

Police chief nods. Mother and daughter hold each other. Police chief leaves. Nusrat suddenly weeps loudly and then stops herself. She takes Benazir's hand.

NUSRAT. We must be brave.

Scene 102

INTERIOR. PRISON, OUTSIDE CELL. NIGHT.

OFFICER (*to Nusrat and Benazir*). I'm sorry. After Death
Sentence no one is allowed in the cell.

*Nusrat and Benazir are stunned. The officer brings forward
two chairs. They sit. Bhutto comes to the door. They talk
through the cell door.*

BHUTTO. Why have both of you come together? Is it
the last time?

NUSRAT. No!

BENAZIR Yes! Yes!

BHUTTO (*shouts to the warder*). Call the Jail Superintendent.
Now!

Warder leaves them alone.

NUSRAT. Zulfy, they could still be bluffing.

BHUTTO. No. I told you from the start they were serious.

NUSRAT (*tears flood her cheeks*). I can't believe it, Zulfy. I
can't.

*She puts her hand through the bars. Bhutto clutches it and
kisses it.*

BHUTTO. Listen carefully. Please, time is short. Benazir,
a lot will depend on you. Never flinch from the

truth. Tell the people that the Generals have killed me because I spoke for the poor. I don't believe that Zia and his gang, even with countless millions of dollars, can hold this country together indefinitely. Five, 10, even 15 years. Then? Then? You will be here Benazir. That will be the time, if the country is still in one piece. You must continue what we started. Finish the job.

BENAZIR. Yes, papa. Yes, yes.

BHUTTO. Your brothers are impulsive. Curb their instincts. No heroism, please. Our time will come again. I came to power on the back of the wave which overthrew the first dictator. New waves will come, that will be the time to act. (*His eyes suddenly fill with tears*) None of us is without faults. You know that better than anyone else. But they are not killing me for my vices, but for my virtues, few though they may have been. That's my message to my people.

Jail Superintendent arrives.

BHUTTO (*cont'd*). Is this the last meeting?

JAIL SUPERINTENDENT. I'm sorry sir (*as he nods*). The death warrant is on my desk.

BHUTTO (*cool, detached*). What time?

JAIL SUPERINTENDENT. At 4.30 a.m., sir. I'm sorry, sir.

Exits.

BENAZIR *(to Warder)*. Please open the door. Let us kiss
my father goodbye.

Warder shakes his head.

BHUTTO. Be brave, my dearest ones. Be brave. Tonight
I'm going back to my own home. I'll become part of
its legend. History. What an unpredictable business.

*He looks at them and smiles. Then lights a cigar. Warder taps
Benazir on the shoulder indicating that their time is up.*

NUSRAT. Zulfy!

BHUTTO. Don't, my darlings. Don't give them any
satisfaction.

*They hold hands through the door. Then the women, looking
at him, leave. He smokes his cigar.*

Scene 103

INTERIOR. DEATH CELL. MIDNIGHT.

Colonel and two other uniformed men enter. Bhutto is sitting on his bed.

BHUTTO. Come to gloat, or watch a murder?

COLONEL. No, no, please Mr Bhutto. I have two papers here. If you will sign them your life will be spared.

Bhutto watches them coldly.

COLONEL *(cont'd)*. The first says you invited the Army to take over. The second accepts your responsibility for the Bangladesh disaster.

BHUTTO *(enraged)*. Shameless bastards. I saved your lot in 1971. You were decimated and destroyed. Should have finished you off.

COLONEL. Your life will be saved.

BHUTTO. I don't want a life of dishonour, lies. Now get out.

COLONEL. It is an order. Sign it.

Two soldiers take Bhutto's hand and try to put the pen into it.

BHUTTO *(shouts)*. Help me, my God. I am innocent!

He grabs Colonel and hits him on the face. Others punch back. Bhutto falls and his head hits the floor. Silence. Colonel bends down, turns Bhutto over on his back. Bhutto is still. Colonel dashes out of the cell.

Scene 104

EXTERIOR. DESERTED STREET. 1.00 A.M.

An Army ambulance is speeding to the prison. It enters the gates, which are closed.

Scene 105

INTERIOR. DEATH CELL. NIGHT.

Bhutto is lying on the ground. Two Army doctors are examining him. Oxygen is being pumped into his lungs. He is given an injection to revive his heart.

Colonel re-enters the cell.

DOCTOR (*to Colonel*). Sorry. No pulse. No blood pressure. He is dead. (*He stands up*) Too bad, eh?

Colonel stares at his colleagues in horror.

Scene 106

EXTERIOR. PRISON COURTYARD. 2.30 A.M.

Some men in civilian clothes are waiting by the gibbet. The Hangman, masked, is standing. From the cells a party of three can be seen in the shadows. Bhutto's body, carried on a stretcher by the two officers, is taken up to the platform.

COLONEL. He's just fainted, but we can't wait.

Hangman takes the body and feels it.

HANGMAN (*to Colonel*). Sir, you have handed me a dead body.

COLONEL. You don't know what you're saying. Hang it anyway.

HANGMAN. Sir, I am not a Muslim but a Christian, as you know. A good and honest hangman. I've done my job for 30 years. My father before me. I cannot hang a dead man.

COLONEL (*taking out a revolver*). Now, good Christian hangman. Do as I say.

Hangman puts a noose around the neck and perfunctorily pulls the rope.

Doctor rushes up to the platform, feels the pulse and nods.

COLONEL. He is dead.

The End.

APPENDIX A

In the matter of

THE LEOPARD AND THE FOX

BY

- TARIQ ALI

OPINION

12.3.86

Bristish Broadcasting Corporation
Broadcasting House
Portland Place
London W1A 1AA

1.*The message*: The essential message of the play is that General Zia and certain of his Generals together with certain of the judges involved in the case participated in the judicial killing of Bhutto. That is no doubt a widely held belief. That and similar allegations were widely made at the time in the international press including the British press and no proceedings were brought. I imagine that no such allegations were made in the newspapers in Pakistan.

The circumstances of the trial and death of Bhutto are highly suspicious and I can understand that there must be a strong temptation to broadcast the play. But suspicions do not constitute evidence. To be more precise, if the defamatory imputation is only that there was reasonable suspicion of guilt, that meaning could be justified by evidence that there were reasonable grounds for suspicion: *Lewis v. Daily Telegraph Ltd.* [1964] AC 234. But I take the play to mean that there was in fact a judicial killing—and not a suspicion of it.

The play can be described as 'faction,' that is to say a dramatised version of actual events. When broadcast by the Corporation, it will be understood, or likely to be understood by reason of the standing of the Corporation, to be an authentic account, and it will be likely to attract worldwide attention and publicity. It may well be that, in the light of the present situation in Pakistan—elections in the offing, and talk of the breakup of Pakistan—General Zia may feel himself to be vulnerable, and we know that the Pakistan High Commission is closely interested in the proposed broadcast. And there are, of course, other potential plaintiffs.

It is necessary, therefore, to consider the position very carefully.

2. *The synopsis*: I cannot set out every aspect of the play: it must be read as a whole. I can only set out a précis.

   1) Owing to unrest in Pakistan, Zia and some of his Generals plot to depose Bhutto.

   2) A Cabinet Minister disclosed to them that Bhutto is about to arrest them and to behead them (2/76).

   3) Zia and a General place Bhutto under house arrest. Zia imposes martial law and promises elections in 90 days and states that he will not deviate from that schedule.

   4) Bhutto is released and is promised that he will be free to campaign in the election period. Bhutto travels to Lahore and is triumphantly received by the people. Zia suggests to Bhutto that he goes to his estates in Larkana and rests, or goes abroad. Bhutto refuses.

   5) Zia and his Generals, excluding Azad, decide that Bhutto is dangerous and must be eliminated and discuss means to execute him, for exam-

ple, charge him with treason before a special military tribunal. (Episode 2: 'One Man One Coffin' and see 2/33–36).

6) Zia appoints his childhood friend, Mushtaq, to be acting Chief Justice and Chief Election Commissioner and Zia becomes Chief Martial Law Administrator.

7) After his meeting with Mushtaq, Zia tells his Generals that Bhutto will be charged with the murder of Raza's father, a three-year-old case which had not been pursued. He overrules his Generals and expresses complete trust in the courts (2/43–45).

8) Bhutto is arrested. Zia postpones the elections for six months. In an interview, Zia says that the courts will decide.

9) Justice Samdani releases Bhutto on bail and refers to the flaws in the case. Zia is angry and orders Bhutto to be re-arrested under Martial Law Regulation No. 12.

10) Public floggings are introduced to frighten the people.

11) The trial. Samdani, who granted bail, is not to sit on the Bench. Mushtaq and another judge exhibit bias against Bhutto and prevent cross-examination of the Prosecution's chief witness.

On a motion held in camera to remove the trial
to another court, Bhutto alleges secret meetings
between Mushtaq and Zia and press conferences
by Mushtaq to foreign journalists; alleges that
the trial is a sham and that Mushtaq is an instrument and that the Army took the decision. The
motion is dismissed and the further trial is held
in camera. There is a unanimous verdict of guilty
and Bhutto is sentenced to death.

12) Bhutto appeals but says that it will be another farce. Two of the appeal judges are said to be
friendly but the others not so.

13) White Papers are prepared on Zia's instruc-
tions. They are said to comprise gossip, hearsay,
innuendo and are vicious. Zia orders a copy to
be sent to each appeal judge. There is also a
daily TV showing of Bhutto's crimes.

14) The appeal. Of the nine appeal judges, two
are 'retired,' one of whom was a 'decent sort.'
Bhutto's lawyer sets out the grounds of appeal
alleging international conspiracy, a thoroughly
hostile and biased Bench and hearsay evidence.
The Chief Justice of the Appeal Court seeks to
influence another judge whose nephew is a senior civil servant. Zia says he wants the appeal
delayed; the Chief Justice says in court that

there is no hurry in conducting the appeal. Zia and the Chief Justice have a private meeting and Zia tells the Chief Justice to tell his fellow judges that he, Zia, has no political ambitions. Bhutto addresses the Appeal Court and alleges that the trial was a farce and vendetta. The Appeal Court decides 4–3 to dismiss the appeal.

15) Bhutto is treated deplorably in prison.

16) Zia ignores world opinion and does not reprieve Bhutto.

17) Bhutto dies in his cell and is nevertheless hanged as an already dead man.

3. *The meaning*: It may be that the play will convey a number of different meanings to different members of the audience. Much may depend upon any nuances conveyed by the way in which the actors play their parts. But the fact that some of the allegations are put into the mouth of, for example, Bhutto does not mean that those allegations do not form part of or contribute to the overall meaning of the play itself.

As I have stated above, the essential message, in my opinion, is of a judicial killing and not merely that there were reasonable grounds for suspecting a judicial killing. The core or the essence of the play can be sum-marised as follows:

1) The decision by Zia and his Generals to eliminate Bhutto. The crucial passages are at 2/33–36 and 2/43–45.

2) Collusion between Zia and Mushtaq to rig the court and to secure a verdict of guilty. This meaning, in my view, can be inferred from:

> i) the fact that Zia appointed Mushtaq as Acting Chief Justice;

> ii) Zia's announcement in the scene following his meeting with Mushtaq to charge Bhutto with murder and

> iii) the fact that Mushtaq was to preside over the Trial Court and that Samdani was not permitted to sit even though he had granted bail.

> iv) The trial was a farce or sham.

> v) Pressure was brought to bear on the Appeal Court.

Those are the ingredients, so to speak, of the charge of judicial killing. They are undoubtedly defamatory allegations.

4. *Who can sue?*

> i) Zia: Depicted as the undoubted ringleader of the plot to secure the elimination of Bhutto, and that allegation is undoubtedly defamatory of him.

ii) The Generals: There were, I understand, seven Generals known to be closely associated with Zia. There were five Generals depicted in the play. Zaman and Nizami are shown as particularly anxious to procure Bhutto's death. Azad is depicted as being reluctant to participate. Although fictitious names are given to the Generals, there will be no difficulty in identifying them with the real-life Generals but I do not know whether there is any internal evidence in the play from which the audience will identify any particular General in the play with any particular real-life General. The allegation that they participated in the plot to eliminate him by whatever means is defamatory of them and I think that all seven Generals could sue.

iii) Mushtaq: The allegations against him are part express and part implied. The express allegations are that he conducted the trial with gross bias against Bhutto and that he secured a conviction on wholly unsatisfactory evidence. The implied or inferential allegations are, or may be, that as appointee of Zia he proposed the three-year-old charge and that he rigged the court by excluding Samdani. Those allegations are all defamatory of him.

iv) The other trial judges: The allegations against them are that they participated in a sham trial; that, by inference, they were guilty of bias and that they reached a verdict on wholly unsatisfactory evidence. Those allegations are defamatory of them. Although they are not named in the play, the names of the real life judges were widely known at the time or at any rate can be easily ascertained now and they would be entitled to sue.

v) Huq: He was known to be the Chief Justice of the Appeal Court in Rawalpindi. The allegation against him is that he sought to bring pressure to bear upon another Appeal Court judge and that he was the presiding judge who upheld a verdict at the end of a trial which was, in effect, a miscarriage of justice.

vi) The three judges: They sided with Huq in dismissing the appeal. Their names are known or can be easily ascertained. The allegation against them is that they upheld a miscarriage of justice and there is the suggestion (though not strongly made) that they succumbed to pressure from Zia in the White Papers and that at least one of them succumbed to pressure by Huq.

Whether any or all of the above persons would be likely to sue is problematic. It is unusual for a head of state to sue but not impossible. And as I have said above, Zia may feel himself now to be in a vulnerable position. It is highly unusual, but not unknown, for a judge to sue—the decision usually depends upon the nature of the allegation made against him. If a judge's integrity and motives are impugned, he may feel obliged to sue. Whether or not a Pakistani judge would sue in England is again problematic. I understand that Mushtaq is in poor health.

There are other allegations defamatory of Zia which I will deal with below (Paragraph 11).

5. *Defences*: I will now consider the possible defences to the 'core' allegations set out in Paragraph 3 above.

6. *Justification*:

i) *The decision to eliminate Bhutto*: The fact of the coup is undisputed. The gist of the plot to eliminate him is contained in 2/33–36, 43–45. The conversations are fictional but will undoubtedly be taken to represent what actually occurred. Although it may have been a widely held belief that Zia and the Generals decided to eliminate Bhutto, that decision is at present only inferential. Would any General be prepared to testify?

Azad is depicted as being reluctant to go ahead with the plot. Is he identifiable with any real-life General? If so, would that General testify? I understand that a General has recently published in Pakistan what might be called a confession. Would he be prepared to testify? If it could be established that Zia and his Generals did in fact plot to eliminate Bhutto, the case would be immeasurably strengthened.

In the absence of direct evidence, it might be pleaded that the decision or plot was to be inferred from all the circumstances. A jury might reach that conclusion—but it would be a highly risky defence: if it failed, the damages could be enormous! Alternatively, it could be contended that the meaning of the play is 'suspicion' of a plot, and that there are reasonable grounds for that suspicion: but, as I have said, I do not think that is the meaning. To justify this allegation is, therefore, fraught with difficulty.

ii) *Collusion between Ziz and Mushtaq*:
   a) To rig the court. It will presumably not be disputed that Zia and Mushtaq were boyhood friends and that Zia appointed Mushtaq as Acting Chief Justice. I understand that Justice Samdani would be prepared to testify,

and I assume that he could say that it was the practice of the Chief Justice to select the court and that he, Samdani and one other judge who also decided the bail application were not appointed to the court, and that it was contrary to practice not to appoint to the court the judges who had heard the bail application.

b) To secure a verdict of guilty. Can we prove that Mushtaq suggested to Zia the case to be brought against Bhutto? Is there any other evidence available to show that there was some collusion between Zia and Mushtaq as to the charge or the verdict? Can a statement be obtained from Justice Samdani? See also (iii) below

iii) *The trial was a farce*: This is, in effect, based upon three allegations:

a) The suggested rigging of the Court. I have dealt with this under (ii) above.

b) Bias. The transcripts of the trial would presumably speak for themselves. But as I understand it, no actual transcripts are available. The fact that bias has been alleged in other publications would not, of itself, prove the truth of the charge. It would be necessary to call the writers if they had been present in court. I understand that Mr John Mathews QC and Mr Ramsey Clarke attended the trial for part of the time as observers. I understand that they will be prepared to testify. Can they give any evidence as to any bias that they witnessed as observers? Are there any other journalists or reporters who attended the trial who will be prepared to testify?

c) The nature and quality of the evidence. The trial went on a long time and the transcripts, even if available which they are not, would be voluminous. Some help may be obtained from the Special Inquiry Tribunal under Shafi ur-Rahman J., who reported in 1975 that Bhutto was not involved in the murder conspiracy, although it would be objected that such evidence was not relevant as it did not, presumably, take into account all the evidence that the Trial Court heard.

Justice Samdani could testify as to the reasons why he granted bail and the flaws that he then saw in the case but, again, it would be objected that he did not hear the whole of the evidence. However, he might be helpful in testifying as to the law of Pakistan in relation to the evidence of 'approvers' and the necessity for corroboration. Has he read the whole of the evidence? Can he say whether or not any requirements of Pakistani law were complied with on such issues?

Mr John Mathews QC and Mr Ramsey Clarke did not sit through the whole trial. But can they give evidence as to the nature and quality of the evidence that they heard?

It is interesting to note that in 2/124 the 'local hacks laugh,' thereby suggesting that the verdict was a foregone conclusion. Are there any journalists or reporters, Pakistani or foreign, who could testify as to the evidence at the trial? The play does not give any real indication of the evidence against Bhutto at the trial and this will be an important point when I come to consider the question of qualified privilege below.

Would any of Bhutto's lawyers be prepared to testify? However, the comment will undoubtedly be made that their evidence would be prejudiced or one-sided.

It may be thought that the judgements of the three dissenting judges in the Appeal Court would be helpful. But that would be no

different from the position of, for example,
Lord Denning who, when dissenting in the
Court of Appeal, usually (but not always)
maintained that he was right.

iv) *Pressure on the appeal court*: This seems to be
based upon three matters—

a) Huq is depicted as 'leaning on' another
Appeal Court judge in relation to the latter's
nephew. Is there any evidence about that?
Can Justice Sansufar Shah give any evidence
about that? Is there any other evidence?

b) Zia ordered White Papers to be prepared.
These are alleged to have been full of gossip
and hearsay, etc. Zia ordered one copy to be
sent to each Appeal Court judge. Can we
obtain copies of the White Papers? No doubt
their contents will speak for themselves. Can
we prove that Zia ordered copies to be sent to
the Appeal Court judges? Can Justice
Sansufar Shah testify as to that? Can Bhutto's
lawyers give any evidence about the appeal?

c) Some help may be obtained from the daily
TV shows showing Bhutto's crimes.

7. *Fair comment*: The subject-matter is, in my opinion,
one of public interest. The 'core' allegations are, in the

main, statements of fact rather than expressions of opinion. In any event, any comment must be based on facts that are truly stated and those facts will be the same or substantially the same as for the plea of justification—depending upon what is complained of as defamatory comment.

8. *Qualified privilege*: A fair and accurate report of English judicial proceedings is protected by qualified privilege. In *Webb Times Publishing Company Limited* (1960) 2 QB 535, a fair and accurate report in England of foreign judicial proceedings was held also to be protected by qualified privilege; but in that case the judicial proceedings (in Switzerland) concerned an Englishman. However, in that case, Pearson, J., said at p. 569:

> One has to look for a legitimate and proper interest as contrasted with an interest which is due to idle curiosity or a desire for gossip . . . There is thus a test available for deciding whether the subject-matter is appropriate for conferring privilege. A report of the decision of the United States Supreme Court on an important question of commercial law has legitimate and proper interest. On the other hand, a report of a judicial proceeding wholly concerned with an alleged scandalous affair between Mrs X and Mr Y is unlikely to have such interest and is likely to appeal only to idle curiosity or a desire for gossip. Sometimes a report of foreign judicial proceedings

will have intrinsic worldwide importance, so that a reasonable man in any civilised country, wishing to be well-informed, will be glad to read it, and would think he ought to read it if he has the time available. Sometimes a report of foreign judicial proceedings will not have such intrinsic worldwide importance, but will have special connection with English affairs, so that it will have a legitimate and proper interest for English readers, and the reasonable man in England will wish to read it or hear about it.

In the present case:

i) Bhutto was Head of State and was known worldwide;

ii) there was worldwide interest in his trial;

iii) Pakistan was formerly a member of the Commonwealth;

iv) there is a large Pakistani population in England;

v) the subject-matter is one of legitimate interest to the public in England, both Pakistani and English, and that interest is not due to 'idle curiosity or a desire for gossip.'

Having considered the matter carefully, I have concluded that this defence would be available for a publication in England and that it should definitely be raised.

It is a necessary requirement that the report be fair and accurate. On the other hand the report cannot set out the whole of the proceedings and may be selective provided that it is neither inaccurate nor unfair to the plaintiff: *Cook v. Alexander* (1974) QB 279; and see per Buckley L. J. at p. 290:

> (The reporter) is I think entitled to report on the proceedings or that part of it which he selects in a manner which fairly and faithfully gives an impression of the events reported and will convey to the reader what he himself would have appreciated had he been present during the proceedings.

See also Duncan and Neill on Defamation, 2nd edition, paragraph 14.29

> Publication of proceedings in camera will not normally be protected by qualified privilege since the proceedings are not by definition in open court. Were any reasons given by the court for sitting in camera? No suggestion appears to have been made that it was necessary to do so in the interests of national security. On the contrary, it seems likely that Mushtaq wished to prevent any reporting of the proceedings (see 2/94) where he is alleged to have stated 'This remark cannot be reported in the press.' If the hearings in camera were contrary to normal procedure I think that what was said in camera and, in particular, Bhutto's speech in his defence would, in the special circumstances of the case, be of legitimate public interest and that publication of the speech or extracts from it would be protected by qualified privilege even though the court had sat in camera.

The play necessarily and inevitably includes only
extracts from the trial and from the appeal. Are those
extracts accurate? It is possible that they would not be
disputed. But if they were disputed, it would be necessary
to consider how they are to be proved to be accurate. As
I understand it there are no transcripts available. Can
witnesses be called such as reporters or journalists who
attended the proceedings? Can Mr John Mathews QC
or Mr Ramsey Clarke testify that the extracts were accurate of the parts of the trial that they heard? Can Justice
Sansufar Shah testify that the extracts from the Appeal
Court are accurate? Can Bhutto's lawyers help?

The report must also be fair. Since extracts are per-
missible, one cannot be expected to cover the whole
trial. On the other hand, there does not appear in the
play to be any real attempt to indicate the substance of
the charges against Bhutto. Did the prosecutor give any
short précis of the nature of the case against Bhutto?
The inclusion of any such extract would go a long way
to indicate a desire not to be unfair to the Plaintiff—
whoever he may be.

9. *Malice*: The defence of fair comment and qualified
privilege can be defeated on proof of malice.
Furthermore, even if those defences are not raised,
proof of malice may tend to aggravate the damages.
The author, Mr Tariq Ali, is a known opponent of the

Zia regime and, as I understand it, is not allowed to enter Pakistan. It is more than likely that an allegation of malice will be made against him. But to establish malice, the Plaintiff (whoever he may be) must prove that the author or the publishers, i.e. the Corporation, published what they knew to be untrue or published the allegations recklessly indifferent as to their truth of falsity, or that their dominant motive was to injure the Plaintiff.

The play reads like an apologia for Bhutto. Of itself there is nothing wrong in that. The only risk is that the author, as a known opponent of Zia, may be alleged to have had as a dominant motive a desire to injure Zia. But proof of malice rests upon the Plaintiff. It is worth quoting the words of Duncan and Neill on Defamation, second edition, paragraph 17.06 (e):

> Even where the defendant did believe the words to be true the plaintiff *may* still be able to prove that the publication was actuated by an improper motive, for example, a desire to injure the plaintiff or to achieve some personal advantage unconnected with the duty or interest which constitutes the reason for the privilege. But in such a case—that is, where the defendant believed the words to be true—judges and juries should be very slow to draw the inference that the sole or dominant motive for publication was the improper motive.

I raise this matter to advert to the risk.

10. *Other defamatory meanings*: In every publication there is a risk that the words will be understood by persons knowing special facts to have some secondary defamatory meaning not apparent on the face of the words. This is a risk which must be borne in mind in the present case since the play is dealing with Pakistani affairs and Pakistani members of the audience may know special facts which are unknown to the Corporation. But this matter cannot be further elaborated or foreseen.

The play does however contain a number of defamatory allegations not included in the 'core' allegations. I will deal with these below.

11. *Zia.* I think that the play contains the following inferences:

> i) That Zia was a hypocrite in his declarations that the courts would decide, while ensuring that the courts found Bhutto guilty. That is defamatory of him. To prove it to be true, it would be necessary to call the same or similar evidence to that to be adduced to justify the 'core' allegations.

> ii) That Zia was a hypocrite in expressing his intention to hold elections in 90 days when in fact he has still not held elections some eight years later. That is defamatory of him. Zia will undoubtedly allege that circumstances changed and it would be difficult if not impossible to jus-

tify the allegation. It may, however, be defensible as a fair comment.

iii) That Zia is a brutal, ruthless dictator. As to that, apart from any evidence available to justify the 'core' allegations, no doubt evidence could be adduced as to the public whippings, shooting at the crowds, etc., and the fact that he did not reprieve Bhutto.

iv) There was, I think, a suggestion that Zia was responsible for the shooting of Mengal's son (1/58 and 2/125–126): I think that the amendments in conference will have avoided, or at any rate substantially reduced, that risk.

12. *General Barnes* (1/16): A fictitious name, but possibly identifiable as a member of the US Defence Intelligence Agency who visited Teheran.

General Shepherd (1/77): May be identifiable as a military attaché at the US Embassy and as one of 'our military advisors.'

Bearing in mind the allegations of United States involvement, for example, an American idea (1/78), the American Embassy in Teheran being very active and Colonel Shepherd visiting GHQ every week (1/90), Americans going too far (1/90), State Department green light to murder (3/20) and 'Americans want me dead' (3/100), any actual person identifiable as General

Barnes or General Shepherd may allege that the allegations of their complicity in the coup and the elimination of Bhutto are defamatory of them. Can it be proved, if necessary, that the allegations are true? I doubt whether any Americans would sue, but it is a possibility.

13. *Princess Ashraf* (1/37): Was known to be an emissary of the Shah of Persia. She is the person aimed at in the original script but the allegation of a drug network is now deleted.

14. *Francoise du Bois*: In the original script she was Lily Savelli. She is now depicted as French (1/41), possibly a representative of the *Sunday Times* (1/48), although that has been amended, and to have interviewed Zia for TV (2/105). Was there a prominent foreign woman journalist who interviewed Zia for TV? If any such person is identifiable, the allegation that she had an affair with Bhutto (1/42, 1/112) will be defamatory of her—unless, of course, the allegation can be proved to be true. The change of name from Lily Savelli to Francoise du Bois will not necessarily obviate the risk. Is it known how many foreign women journalists interviewed Zia for TV? If they are all identifiable, they might all be able to sue.

15. *Bhutto 'surrounded himself with gangsters, sycophants, time-servers'* (1/47): This is a general allegation. Khalid and Akbar are described in the play as Cabinet Ministers close to Bhutto and may, therefore, be identi-

fiable with real persons. Rashid is described as Bhutto's political advisor and may, likewise, be identifiable with a real person. Any persons so identifiable may complain that in the context they will be understood to be 'gangsters, sycophants, time-servers.' There is also a stage direction requiring Khalid and Akbar to look at Bhutto 'with admiration' (1/137). Perhaps an amendment to 'some of his supporters were gangsters, sycophants, time-servers' will help to reduce the risk, but will not, I think, eliminate it altogether.

16. *The woman caught stealing panties at Marks and Spencers* (1/81): she was well known in Pakistan as the wife of Wali Khan and will be identifiable to some members of the audience. She may complain that 'characteristic self-delusion,' etc., will be understood to mean that her protestations of innocence were not genuine and the implication that she was insincere and that she was rightly convicted are defamatory of her. However, if it can be proved that she was, in fact, convicted, her conviction will be conclusive evidence that she committed the offence: Civil Evidence Act 1968 s. 13(1). However if she was fined, the conviction would be spent after five years: Rehabilitation of Offenders Act 1974 s. 5 Table A, and she could sue if the publication was proved to have been made with malice: s. 8(4). The further allegation of some impropriety on her part is now deleted.

17. *One Arab ambassador 'pimping' for the Opposition* (1/90): Is the Ambassador identifiable? Was an Arab ambassador known to be siding with the Opposition? If so, he may complain that to describe him as 'pimping' is defamatory.

18. *A Cabinet Minister (1/142) whose name is not deleted (2/76) but who is alleged to have betrayed to Zia and his Generals the information that Bhutto was about to arrest and behead them (2/76):* I understand that there were 22 Cabinet Ministers. The difficult question arises as to whether each Cabinet Minister could claim to be identified, or whether the class is too wide. For myself, I think that the class is too wide and that all 22 Cabinet Ministers could not claim to be identified. However, I concede that there is a risk. In the final analysis, whether or not all 22 are reasonably identifiable is a question of impression. There may, however, be some fact or facts in the play or known to some members of the audience which would serve to identify one particular Cabinet Minister as the minister involved. I do not know whether there is or are any such fact or facts. If necessary, could it be proved that a Cabinet Minister did disclose this information to Zia and his collaborators?

19. *Habib (3/35–38) is identifiable as Rahim:* I doubt whether this passage is defamatory of Rahim unless he complains that it means that

(i) that he was a traitor to Bhutto; or

(ii) that he was one of the 'gangsters, sycophants, time servers' close to Bhutto and was ill-
treated for being so.

I understand that Mr Rahim will be asked to approve
the passage as accurate and true of himself.

20. All the above characters in paragraphs 12 to 19
inclusive (excepting Princess Ashraf, reference to whom
is now deleted) are peripheral to the 'core' of the play.
Nevertheless, if they are identifiable with real life persons, as I have indicated, there is a potential risk, to a
greater or less extent, that one or other or all may sue.

21. *Damages.*

i) The 'core.' If Zia or any Generals or judges
sue in relation to the defamatory allegations
which represent the core of the play, and any
defences fail, for example, because justification
cannot be proved, or because any plea of qualified privilege in relation to the court scenes fails
because the reports are not fair and accurate or
because the privilege is defeated on proof of
malice, the damages could be very substantial.
There is also a possibility that aggravated damages might be awarded in the light of the
author's known views of Zia and the regime.

However, the core allegations were published in
the British and international press, and it may

be possible to plead, in mitigation of damages, that the Plaintiffs, whether Zia or the Generals or the judges, have acquired a bad reputation.

ii) The peripheral allegations. We have tried, by amendments, to lessen the risk of these. But there is always a risk. The damages would not, however, be so high as they would be in relation to the core allegations.

22. *Conclusion*: I have endeavoured to point to the risks involved in broadcasting this play. It is impossible to forecast whether any and if so which of the central or peripheral characters might sue in England. As I have said, the core allegations appear already to have been published in the newspapers in Britain and elsewhere without complaint. But a dramatised play will undoubtedly create an impact. It seems to me that, in the final analysis, it must be a policy decision as to whether or not to broadcast the play. As I have stated, it may balance the play to give some indication in the trial of the case made against Bhutto. I do not have any information about that—and, of course, it only goes to one aspect of the play.

A T Hoolahan QC
1 Brick Court
Temple EC4
10th March 1986

APPENDIX B

From: Deputy Solicitor

417, 16 Lang St.   2423   5.2.86

Subject: *The Leopard and the Fox*

To: Robin Midgley (H. D. Tel. Pebble Mill) &
    Keith Williams

Copy to: C.BBC-2; H.N.P.C. (David Waine);
    D. P. Tel.

I have read with interest your memo of 29th January.

I think it would be helpful following our earlier discussion to summarise the law which would be applied
were libel actions provoked by the defamations in the
present scripts.

It would be no part of a Plaintiff's case to prove that the defamatory words, i.e. those damaging his or her character or reputation, are false. The law presumes it in his or her favour. But, it is a complete defence to an action for libel that the defamatory imputation is true. Such a plea in the defence that the words are true is called a Plea of Justification. To make good the plea, the Defendant must prove that the imputation is true, not merely that he believes it to be true. For example, if I say of the Plaintiff that I believe he committed murder, I cannot justify it by saying and proving I did believe it. Again, if I were to repeat a rumour I could not say it is true by proving that the rumour existed. I would have to prove that the subject matter of the rumour was true. The Defendant has, therefore, to justify the sting of the precise charge complained of.

If the libel contains defamatory statements both of fact and opinion, the Defendant, under a Plea of Justification, must prove that the statements of fact are true and that the statements of opinion are correct.

A good defence is also available to a Defendant to prove that the words complained of are no more than fair and honest comment on a matter of public interest. If, therefore, the facts are truly stated with regard to a matter of public interest, the Defendant will succeed in this defence if the jury are satisfied that the comments are fairly and honestly made. This defence will not fail by reason only that the truth of every allegation of fact is not proved, provided the expression of opinion is fair comment having regard to such facts alleged or referred to in the words complained of as are proved to be true. Subject to that, it is incumbent upon the Defendant under a plea of fair comment to prove (a) that each and every statement of fact in the words complained of is true, and (b) that the comment on the facts so proved was bona fide and fair comment on a matter of public interest. The comments must not mis-state facts because a comment cannot be fair which is built upon facts which are not truly stated.

A clear distinction, therefore, exists between comment or criticism and allegation of fact, such as, that despicable conduct has taken place. It is one thing to comment upon the private acts of a public man, and quite another to assert that he had been guilty of particular acts of misconduct.

The fair comment defence can be defeated by the Plaintiff proving malice on the part of the Defendant, for example, if a writer through unreasonable prejudice has allowed himself to cast reckless aspersions on the Plaintiff which, but for his state of mind, he could not have honestly believed. If it can be proved that out of an unreasonable prejudice the Defendant has stated as true that which he does not know to be true, or has stated it without taking the trouble to ascertain whether it is true or not, a jury might infer that the mind of the Defendant was actuated by malice against the Plaintiff.

In referring to Counsel in our discussion, what I was intending to say to you was that I was satisfied that any Counsel instructed in connection with libel proceedings brought as a result of the present scripts would identify the same defamatory aspects as I had pointed out to you and the same defences as available. Were such proceedings to be brought the papers would in fact be referred to a specialist libel counsel.

The present scripts do contain a substantial amount of defamatory material to which the defences outlined above would have to be applied. The main potential Plaintiffs could be:

1) Zia

2) Mrs Zia

3) Some if not all of the judges concerned in the trials

4) James Callaghan

5) Mr Bakhtiar

6) Mr Abdul Hafeez Prizada (Khalid), Mr Mumtaz Ali Bhutto (Akbar), Shaikh Mohammad Rashid (Rashid), Maulana Kausar Naizi (Maulana Whiskey), and other established

close associates of Bhutto, particularly those in his Cabinet of March 1977 (the members of which are listed in the attached extract from *The Times*) who could be classified from the scripts as 'pimps, gangsters, sycophants and time-servers.'

7) A Sheik or Sheiks who had Ambassadorial accreditation to the Government of Pakistan in 1978/79.

8) The Intercontinental Hotel in Karachi.

9) The sister of the late Shah of Persia

At our meeting I also pointed out to you that the use of fictional names was no protection if real-life persons could identify with the characters in the roles.

I also hope that I made clear the danger of the invented conversation. It is no defence to argue that such conversation probably had taken place, or that in any event, in the opinion of the author, that conversation accurately reflected the history of the matter. The facts and opinions expressed in such conversations must meet the requirements of the defences mentioned earlier. There is no defence of dramatic licence. Further, the device of the invented conversation could result in a successful Plaintiff being awarded aggravated damages.

I believe we agreed that the play was very much a political statement, and that careful appraisal would have to be given to the evidence of witnesses produced with a view to sustaining the charges which the play makes against individuals. We might, for example, have to face the argument that those witnesses were persons disaffected from the Zia regime, or banned from their home country, with partisan motives of their own for discrediting Zia and the military government. The author, for example, has since 1977 chosen not to return to his country, Pakistan, and his parents have suffered imprisonment in Lahore during the interim at the hands of the present regime. I also understand that Zia has personally attacked the author's book *Can Pakistan Survive?* (Penguin: 1983).

On the two trials in Lahore and Rawalpindi, I have read a great deal. The Lahore hearing in its public conduct seems in both the partisan and neutral reporting to be exposed to a good deal of criticism. The Rawalpindi hearing, however, is less criticised. Indeed, neither Professor Wolf Phillips nor Victoria Schofield, a close friend of the Bhutto family, in her book *Bhutto: Trial and Execution* (Cassell: 1979) charges Zia or the Chief Justice in Rawalpindi with the specific conduct alleged in the play. Indeed, as regards Zia, Victoria Schofield admits that he had his own share of rumours levelled at him. 'No-one quite knew,' she writes 'what was happening and so fantastic ideas were put forward.'

With regard to your reference to Mr Justice Samdani, he heard Bhutto's bail application when Bhutto was charged, not when he had been convicted and condemned. Samdani had, in fact, no direct involvement in either the Lahore or Rawalpindi trials. He may have been a spectator.

I note what you say regarding Mr Justice Safdar Shar. He was certainly one of the three dissenting Judges of the Rawalpindi Appeal Court. From your memorandum I am assuming that he is the 'Tall Judge' introduced at page 63 of episode 3. I am not informed as to the nature of the record of his conversation with Chief Justice Anwarul Haq. The form that the record takes would have to be a matter for assessment evidentially. (The 'Tall Judge' also states that Mr Bakhtiar is a bad lawyer!)

A major problem is that most of the dramatis personae are still alive. Insofar as the script defames them by statement of fact or opinion, then the BBC in publishing those statements and opinions can only rely on the defences which I have outlined were defamation proceedings to be brought. It is really not possible to assist you with a forecast as to the probability of proceedings. That, in the end, must be a matter for editorial judgement. But were proceedings brought we might have to fight off the charge by the Plaintiffs in the words of W. S. Maugham in 'The Summing Up' that 'the drama is make believe. It does not deal with truth (in the evidential sense) but with effect.'

I enclose for your information a copy of a report by Chris Sherwell in *The Financial Times* of 5th April 1979 which you may find of interest, together with a copy article from *The Times* of 31st March 1977 listing the new Bhutto Cabinet on which I have highlighted the real-life politicians who appear to figure in the scripts.

I have also had the advantage of reading *Can Pakistan Survive* by the author of the scripts. In that book he does not choose to dwell in any detail upon the trials. While he states that the Pakistan judiciary was not known for its impartiality, he is careful in an end note to the chapter containing that remark to state, 'We do not intend to suggest that all Pakistan judges were willing tools of successive regimes. There were honourable exceptions throughout Pakistan's history.'

J. P. Coman

AS/encs.